A Virginia Military Institute Album, 1839-1910

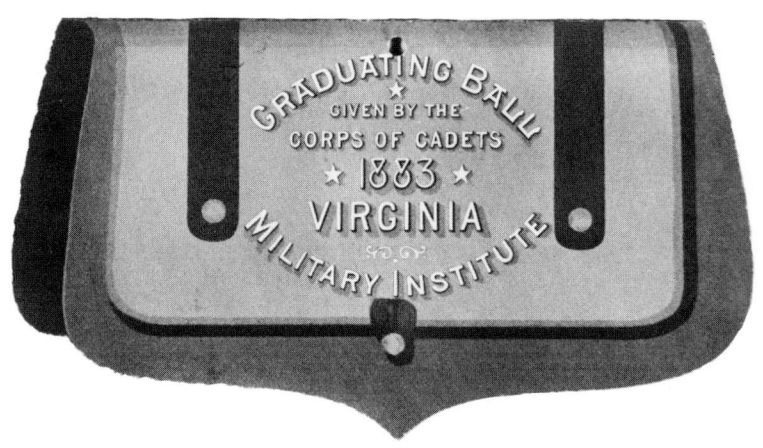

Parade in Lexington, c. 1903

A Virginia Military Institute Album, 1839–1910

A Collection of Photographs and Manuscripts from
the VMI Archives, Lexington, Virginia

Diane B. Jacob and Judith Moreland Arnold

Published for
the Friends of Preston Library
by the University Press of Virginia
Charlottesville

THE UNIVERSITY PRESS OF VIRGINIA
Copyright © 1982 by the Friends of
Preston Library

First published 1982

Library of Congress Cataloging in Publication Data
Main entry under title:
A Virginia Military Institute album, 1839–1910.

1. Virginia Military Institute—History—Sources. I. Jacob, Diane B. II. Arnold, Judith Moreland.
U430.V8V53   378.755′853   82-1865
ISBN 0-8139-0947-3   AACR2

Printed in the United States of America

Front cover: Cadets and townspeople in front of William J. Hubard's Washington Statue, c. 1866–67. Dedicated in 1856, this bronze casting of Houdon's original was the first statue at VMI. General David Hunter's Union forces carried it to West Virginia after burning the Institute in June 1864. It was returned following the war and rededicated in September 1866.

Front endleaf: Dress parade, c. 1880

Back endleaf: Entrance to VMI, c. 1889

Back cover: Advertisement from *The Bomb*, 1885

for Colonel William Couper (1884–1964)

Class of 1904, VMI Business Executive, and VMI Historiographer. His interest in VMI's heritage ensured the survival of the materials contained in this book.

Football action, 1893

The Washington Arch facade of Barracks, May 15, 1876. Drawn by Cadet Thomas W. Keitt

Special Acknowledgments

The publication of this book was made possible by Mr. and Mrs. Solon B. Turman of New Orleans, Life members of the Friends of Preston Library. Mr. Turman is a member of the Class of 1920, a recipient of the VMI Foundation's Distinguished Service Award, and for many years has been one of the Institute's most generous donors.

The project also received the support of the VMI Foundation, Inc. and the Friends of Preston Library, an organization founded in 1978 to bridge the gap between state financial support and actual library needs for collections, services, and facilities.

Finally, nothing could have been done without the archivists' familiarity with the materials in the Archives, from which this small portion of photographs and documents was skillfully selected. Diane B. Jacob and Judith M. Arnold have our thanks for creating this handsome new addition to VMI's published histories.

JAMES E. GAINES, JR.
Head Librarian

Rifle volley in old Cadet Cemetery, c. 1900

Preface

Photographs are timeless. As visual links between past and present, they not only show us how much things have changed but also reflect the continuity in our lives and in human nature. Anyone who has spent an evening browsing through an old photograph album is aware of the mixed emotions that the images evoke. Photographs capture forever moments in our lives, and when we reexamine those moments we are often startled by the picture of the past as it really was, uncolored by nostalgia and faulty memory. In this way, photographs are unique historical records, enabling us to view ourselves with a clarity that can be both disconcerting and amusing.

This volume is like any other family album. It brings into focus a specific place and time—the Virginia Military Institute from its founding in 1839 through the first decade of the twentieth century. Many of the names and events that appear on the following pages will be familiar to cadets, alumni, and to residents of Lexington; most of the photographs and manuscripts that we have used to bring these names and events to life will be unfamiliar. But these pages illustrate more than the history of a military college. In sifting through the hundreds of photographs in VMI's collection, we were captivated by the images, by their ability to explain our present as well as our past. These photographs reflect that part of the human spirit which can endure difficulties, whether they be as trivial as an examination or as shattering as war and the death of close friends. They also remind us what it is like to be young, to find strength in friendship and humor in unpleasant circumstances.

The photographs in this book were selected from a collection of over 3,000 images for their quality of composition, subject matter, historical significance, and human interest. Many of the nineteenth-century photographs were taken by Lexington's noted photographer Michael Miley. Miley's life and work are outlined in a fine essay by Mame Warren, which we have included as an appendix. Our decision to end the album with 1910 was influenced by the decline in the quality and variety of the photographs after this date and by our desire to cover the era of VMI's first two superintendents, Francis H. Smith and Scott Shipp. Both men determined the pattern of cadet life and guided the Institute through some of its most glorious and its most troubled years. To complement the photographs, we have chosen original manuscripts and excerpts from cadet letters and diaries. The legends identify the illustrations and their dates; additional information, such as the size of the original photograph, photographer, and accession number or location in the Archives, may be found in the Key to Illustrations and Quotations.

Rather than forcing the photographs into arbitrary categories, we let the images dictate the structure of the book. As we were making the final selection of the photographs to be included, we saw that they fell easily into three natural divisions which in turn determined the content of our three chapters. "Faces from the Past: The Old Corps" contains individual and group portraits, illustrates the significance of a cadet's membership in a class and in the Corps, and covers the Civil War, Robert E. Lee's funeral, and the other unique events that interrupted the everyday life of the Corps. "Reveille to Taps," which depicts the military and academic routine, also includes a section devoted to early faculty members. "Team Spirit, Calics, and 'Frolics after Taps'" features early athletic teams and events, social life, and the variety of "illegal" (forbidden by the regulations) activities that cadets have cheerfully indulged in since the day VMI opened its doors in 1839. We have also provided a brief introduction for those unfamiliar with the origin of the Institute.

Our intention has been to convey the essence of life at the Institute through a limited selection of photographs and original documents, not to create a comprehensive history of VMI. Readers interested in a detailed account are referred to Colonel William Couper's *One Hundred Years at VMI*. Similarly, while we have used photographs of many buildings and have made a particular effort to include structures that no longer exist, we have not attempted to duplicate the recent work of Royster Lyle and Pamela Hemenway Simpson. Their *Architecture of Historic Lexington* is the best source for those interested in learning more about VMI's architecture.

We are indebted to many for their interest, support, and advice: those who have donated items to the VMI Archives; J. H. Binford Peay, Jr. (Chairman of the Friends of Preston Library); Joseph D. Neikirk; Lt. Colonel James E. Gaines, Jr., Helen T. Cox, Wylma P. Davis, Betty T. Hamric, Elizabeth S. Hostetter, John M. Robson, and the other members of the Preston Library staff; Brig. Gen. James M. Morgan, Jr.; former Superintendent Richard L. Irby; Julia S. Martin; Keith E. Gibson; June F. Cunningham; Larry I. Bland; and Royster Lyle, Jr. We are grateful to Mame Warren and Washington and Lee University for their permission to reprint Ms. Warren's essay on Michael Miley. A special note of thanks goes to Michael Collingwood of André Studio, Inc. in Lexington, who brought many fragile and imperfect photographs back to life.

Camp scene, c. 1890

Contents

Preface	ix
Introduction: From Arsenal to Institute	1
Faces from the Past: The Old Corps	6
Reveille to Taps	37
Team Spirit, Calics, and "Frolics after Taps"	68
Appendix: Michael Miley, 1841–1918, *by Mame Warren*	92
Key to Illustrations and Quotations	96
Name Index	98

Samuel M. Lawrason, c. 1872

A Virginia Military Institute Album, 1839–1910

PLEDGE.

I hereby engage to serve as a Cadet in the Virginia Military Institute for the term for which I have entered, and I promise on honour while I continue a member thereof to obey all legal orders of the Constituted Authorities of the Institute, and to discharge all my duties as Cadet with regularity and fidelity. (And if a State-Cadet), I further promise to serve as Teacher in some one of the schools of the Commonwealth for the term of two years after finishing my course, unless excused by the Board of Visitors.

Limit Gates, 1889

Introduction: From Arsenal to Institute

On March 29, 1839, the Virginia legislature passed the final version of an act that established a military school at the site of the State Arsenal in Lexington. This vote of approval was the result of years of heated debate among state legislators and many of the prominent citizens of Lexington. The governor appointed a Board of Visitors to oversee the new "Virginia Military Institute," and they elected as president of the Board Claudius Crozet, a native of France who was educated at the prestigious École Polytechnique, had served in Napoleon's army, had taught engineering at West Point, and in 1839 was principal engineer of Virginia. Francis Henney Smith, a young West Point graduate and professor of mathematics at Hampden-Sydney College, was offered and accepted the position of "Principal Professor" (his title was later changed to superintendent) at the new school. Both Crozet and Smith drew on past experience when faced with the task of organizing the Institute, so it was natural that West Point's regulations and uniform were adapted for use at VMI. Preparations were made to begin classes in the fall, and on November 11, 1839, the first group of cadets reported to Smith and officially replaced the Arsenal Guard.

"Said school shall be called the 'Virginia Military Institute.'" From An Act amending & reducing into one the several Acts concerning the reorganization of the Lexington Arsenal, and the establishment therewith of a Military School, March 29, 1839

> "I have just returned from exploring the dusky halls of the old Arsenal. There are deposited in this arsenal at which we are stationed, fifty six thousand stand of arms including a vast number of old rifles, muskets, pistols and Dragoon swords. The value of the whole is estimated at about seven hundred thousand dollars so you see we have great responsibility resting upon us."

Cadet Valentine C. Saunders to his parents, November 30, 1839. Saunders received his diploma on July 4, 1842, along with fifteen other members of VMI's first graduating class.

This early view of VMI shows the original Barracks in the center with the Arsenal Building directly behind (lithograph, 1847). All of the structures in this view had been razed by the time of the Civil War.

> The Virginia Military Institute went into operation a few days since, under the superintendance of Major Smith.—John T. L. Preston, Esq., of this place, was elected by the Board Professor of Modern Languages—French and German—for one year. Mr. P. is an intelligent gentleman, of fine education, and will, we hope, make an acceptable Professor. Major Smith and *we* having served together in Uncle Sam's army at West Point, we can testify that he there sustained a high character, both for soldiership and scholarship. The institution could not well be in better hands.

4

Lexington Gazette, November 30, 1839. John T. L. Preston was one of the strongest advocates of the movement to convert the Arsenal into a state military school. As a member of the original board of Visitors, he assumed the role of spokesman for the group in his letters to Francis H. Smith. The correspondence contains early "unofficial" statements regarding the school's organization and philosophy.

5

Francis H. Smith (1812–1890), VMI's first superintendent (c. 1862). Smith, an 1833 West Point graduate, would guide the Institute through its first half century.

"He is our only son, who was sorely afflicted by illness in his early youth, & may therefore have been more indulged than was proper. If the partiality of a parent does not mislead me, I think you will not find him deficient in capacity, or I trust in laudable ambitions.... I submit him to your guidance with the utmost confidence... that every proper attention will be paid to his intellectual & moral culture."

William Browne, father of Cadet William T. Browne, to Francis H. Smith, July 11, 1841

Cadet of the 1850s. The Arsenal Act of March 29, 1839, gave the Board of Visitors the power "to admit as the regular students or cadets ... any number of young men not fewer than twenty, nor exceeding forty, and who shall not be less than sixteen nor more than twenty five years of age; and in this admission to [be] made upon undoubted evidence of fair moral character, a strict regard shall be had to the proportionate population of the four great constitutional divisions of the State."

> "As a place of residence, I should hope you would find Lexington agreeable, as the population is intelligent, moral, & religious."

John T. L. Preston to Francis H. Smith, April 29, 1839

Lexington viewed from Institute Hill, c. 1875. The Guard Tree, near which the guard tent was pitched during summer encampment, stands on the Parade Ground at the far right.

Faces from the Past:

The Corps of Cadets, April 26, 1869

The Old Corps

FROM the time a new cadet, or "rat," registers at VMI, he becomes a member of a class and of the Corps of Cadets. The traditions of class solidarity and loyalty to the Corps were shaped by the young men who appear on the following pages. They witnessed the Institute's early years, its destruction in war, and its rebuilding.

A list of the first cadets to enter VMI, November 11, 1839

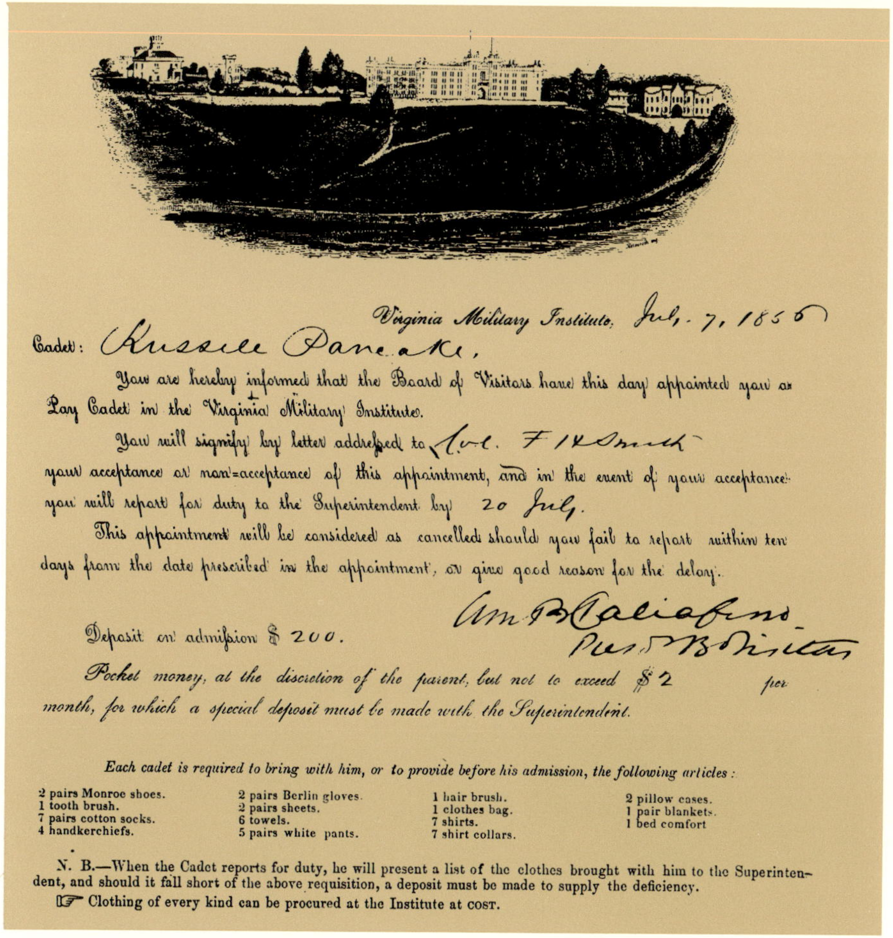

Virginia Military Institute, July 7, 1856

Cadet: Russell Pancake,

You are hereby informed that the Board of Visitors have this day appointed you a Pay Cadet in the Virginia Military Institute.

You will signify by letter addressed to Col. F H Smith your acceptance or non-acceptance of this appointment, and in the event of your acceptance you will report for duty to the Superintendent by 20 July.

This appointment will be considered as cancelled should you fail to report within ten days from the date prescribed in the appointment, or give good reason for the delay.

Deposit on admission $ 200.

Wm B Taliaferro
Prest B Visitors

Pocket money, at the discretion of the parent, but not to exceed $2 per month, for which a special deposit must be made with the Superintendent.

Each cadet is required to bring with him, or to provide before his admission, the following articles:

2 pairs Monroe shoes.	2 pairs Berlin gloves.	1 hair brush.	2 pillow cases.
1 tooth brush.	2 pairs sheets.	1 clothes bag.	1 pair blankets.
7 pairs cotton socks.	6 towels.	7 shirts.	1 bed comfort
4 handkerchiefs.	5 pairs white pants.	7 shirt collars.	

N. B.—When the Cadet reports for duty, he will present a list of the clothes brought with him to the Superintendent, and should it fall short of the above requisition, a deposit must be made to supply the deficiency.

☞ Clothing of every kind can be procured at the Institute at COST.

11

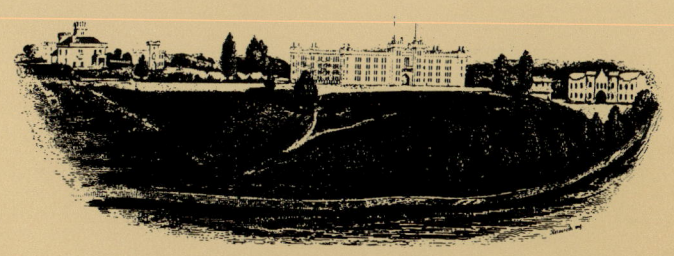

An early letter of appointment to VMI (July 7, 1856). New cadets were expected to report in person to Superintendent Smith.

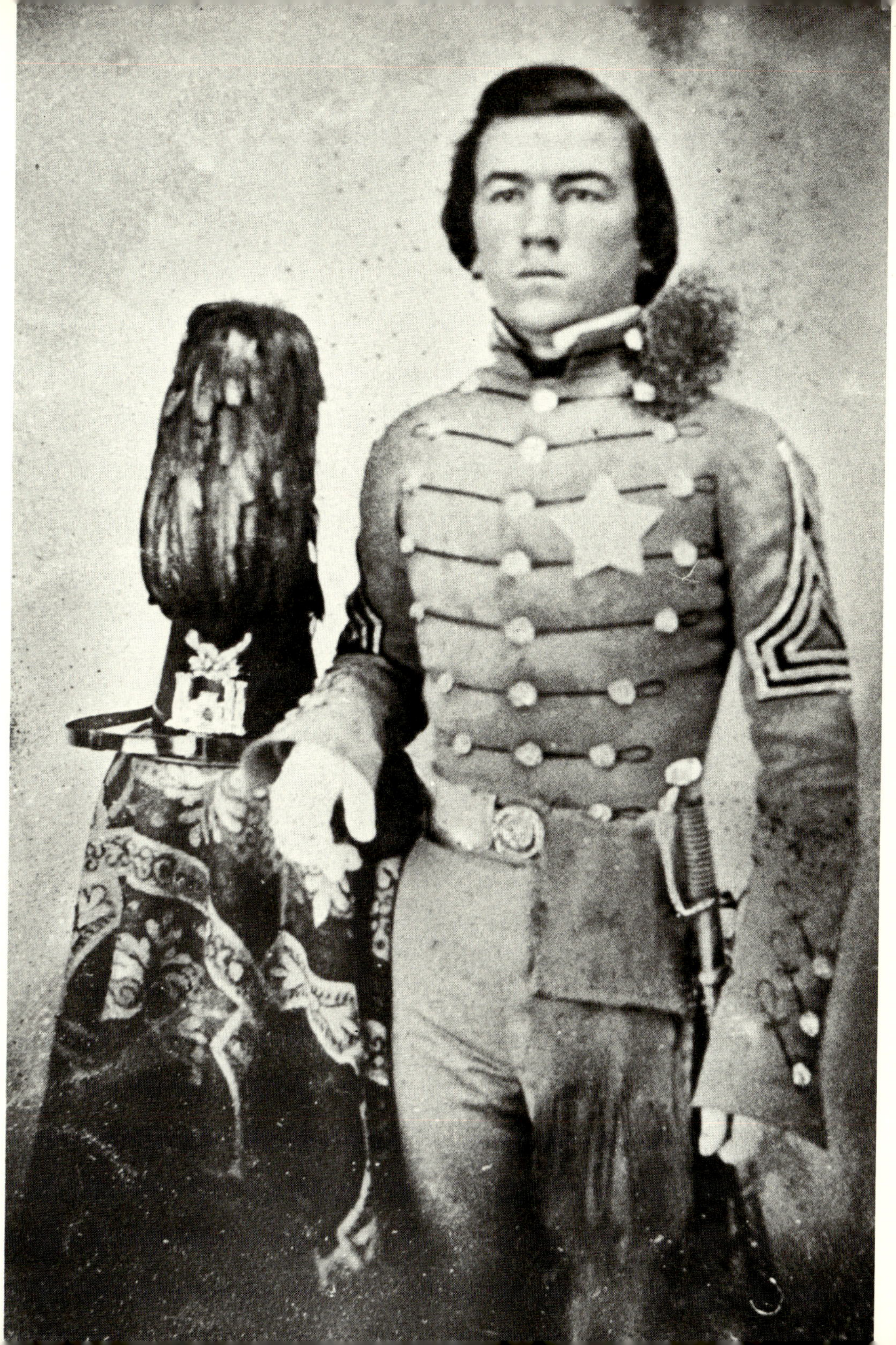

12

Cadet Charles W. Hardy, c. 1857

14

Superintendent's order stipulating arrangement of furniture in Barracks rooms, April 12, 1840

13

"Friday night. 8½ O'Clock. Mch. 16th 55. No. 14." Drawing of Barracks room by Cadet James H. Waddell (March 1855)

Cadets Edward B. Goode and Waller M. Boyd, c. 1860

"The enemy are hovering upon our borders."

From superintendent's order to aid General Jackson, May 1, 1862

1859 November	A contingent of the Corps was dispatched to Charlestown following John Brown's raid on the Harpers Ferry arsenal. Cadets stood guard at Brown's execution on December 2.
1861 April	The Corps was sent to Richmond, where cadets drilled Confederate army recruits. The commanding officer during this trip was Major Thomas J. (later General Stonewall) Jackson, who had joined VMI's faculty in 1851 as professor of natural and experimental philosophy and instructor of artillery. Jackson accepted a commission and left for active duty soon after the Corps arrived in Richmond.
1862 May	The Corps was ordered to aid General Jackson's forces during the McDowell campaign. The cadets, commanded by Scott Shipp, marched in pursuit of Federal troops but were not engaged in battle.
1863	General Stonewall Jackson died on May 10 from wounds received at the Battle of Chancellorsville, and his body was returned to Lexington for burial. Later this year (August–December), the Corps was called to defend against the raids of General William Averell.
1864 May 15	The Battle of New Market. The Corps, again under the command of Scott Shipp, marched into battle along with General John C. Breckinridge's forces against Federal troops led by General Franz Sigel. Ten cadets were mortally wounded: Samuel Francis Atwill, William Henry Cabell, Charles Gay Crockett, Alva Curtis Hartsfield, Luther Cary Haynes, Thomas Garland Jefferson, Henry Jenner Jones, William Hugh McDowell, Jaqueline Beverly Stanard, and Joseph Christopher Wheelwright.
1864 June 11	Federal troops, under the command of General David Hunter, entered Lexington. The Corps retreated to a camp in the Blue Ridge near Balcony Falls. VMI was burned the next day by Hunter's soldiers. On June 25 the Corps returned to Lexington, only to be furloughed two days later.
1864 December	Academic work resumed at the Alms House in Richmond, VMI's temporary headquarters.
1865 April	Richmond was evacuated and the Corps disbanded. The Confederacy surrendered at Appomattox.
1865 October	VMI reopened in Lexington.

16

Scott Shipp (c. 1867), an 1859 VMI graduate, served as the Institute's commandant of cadets from 1862 to 1889 and as its second superintendent from 1890 to June 1907. He commanded the Corps during the McDowell campaign and at the Battle of New Market.

> "It is the painful duty of the Superintendent to announce to the Corps of Cadets the death of their late comrade, Cadet John T. Gisiner. He died at the residence of his father on Saturday last—impressively admonishing all of the shortness and uncertainty of life."

Superintendent's order, June 13, 1862

Cadet John T. D. Gisiner (1862) died in June 1862 from an illness contracted during the Corps's participation in the McDowell campaign.

FUNERAL OF LIEUT. GENERAL T. J. JACKSON.

All that was mortal of our great and good chief, Lieut. Gen. T. J. Jackson was consigned to the tomb on Friday last.

The body having reached Lexington by the Packet boat on Thursday afternoon, accompanied by his personal staff, Maj. A. S. Pendleton, Surgeon, H. McGuire, Lieut. Morrison and Lieut. Smith, by his Excellency Gov. Letcher, and a delegation of the citizens of Lynchburg; it was received by the Corps of Cadets and escorted to the Institute, and deposited in his late Lecture Room, which had been appropriately draped in mourning. There was the table used by the late Professor—the same chair in which he sat—the cases with the Philosophical apparatus he had used—all told of his quiet and unobtrusive labors in his Professional life—and placed just as he left them, when he received the order of the Governor of Virginia, to march the Corps of Cadets to Richmond, on the 20th April, 1861. He left the Va. Military Institute in command of the Cadets. He has been brought back to sleep among us—a world renowned christian Hero. The procession moved from the Institute on Friday morning at 10 A. M. The Funeral escort was commanded by Maj. S. Ship, Commandant of Cadets, a former pupil of Gen. Jackson and a gallant officer who had served with him in his Valley Campaign, as Major of the 21st Va. Reg't.

18

Lexington Gazette, May 20, 1863

19

Sketch of General Thomas J. ("Stonewall") Jackson by Moses Ezekiel. Ezekiel, a New Market cadet who became a noted sculptor, created two major works of art for VMI. Virginia Mourning Her Dead, *a monument dedicated to the cadets who died in the Battle of New Market, was unveiled in 1903, and in 1912 his statue of Stonewall Jackson was dedicated.*

Women mourning at Jackson's grave, c. 1866–70

> "Sorrow shrieks, and memory wails, when I revert to the bloody picture of intolerable scenes of suffering and destruction which encompassed me on every side.... 'War is a hard thing!' Five of the bodies of my comrades who fell in that action have been brought here and re-interred in a vault just in rear of the institute building."

New Market Cadet John L. Tunstall to his mother, May 15, 1866

21

"Cadet Stanard's body is at New Market I presume" (May 16, 1864). *Jaqueline Beverly Stanard was one of the ten cadets who were mortally wounded at the Battle of New Market.*

22

Five veterans of the Battle of New Market, c. 1866–67. Clockwise from upper left: Cadets Hardaway H. Dinwiddie, Gaylord B. Clark, Thomas G. Hayes, John L. Tunstall, and Edward M. Tutwiler. *All were members of the Class of 1867.*

23

The old Cadet Cemetery (c. 1900) was established in 1878 near what is now the northwest corner of the Parade Ground. The bodies of five of the cadets killed at New Market were buried here until 1912, when they were reinterred beneath Ezekiel's monument.

24

Virginia Mourning Her Dead *by Moses Ezekiel (1903)*

"Yankee thieves and incendiaries"

VMI Surgeon Robert L. Madison's description of Hunter's troops, July 1, 1864

25

Crowd gathered in front of the ruins of Barracks for the ceremony to rededicate the Washington Statue, September 10, 1866

"This is a nice place. There is about 6 thousand inhabitants and the buildings are good. There was a milatry school here but we have burnt all the buildings. It was a pitty to do it but I suppose it could not be helpt."

Union soldier Sidney Marlin to his wife, June 14, 1864

"I suppose of course that you have all read full accounts of Gen. Lee's death in the papers. He died on the morning of the 12th at about half past nine. All business was suspended at once all over the country and town, and all duties military & academic suspended at the Institute, and all the black crape . . . in Lexington was used up at once. . . . Every cadet had black crape issued to him. . . . The battallion flag was heavily draped in black. . . . The Institute has been hung all around with black. . . .

"Some days before he was taken I met him in the path leading into town, coming in [the] direction of the barracks. He was walking, and seemed to be the picture of health, and when I saw him in his coffin, he looked to be reduced to half his original size, and desperately thin. . . . Myself and four other cadets with Gen. Smith's permission sat up all night with the corpse on Friday night, perfect silence was kept the whole night, no one speaking except in a low whisper. It was considered a great honor to be allowed to sit up with the remains."

Cadet William Nalle to his mother, October 16, 1870

Robert E. Lee, c. 1870. Lee came to Lexington after the war to serve as president of Washington College. Because of the proximity of the two schools, he was a familiar figure to VMI cadets. When Lee died in October 1870, they mourned the loss of both a military hero and a respected member of their community.

27

Tall and short, c. 1870

28

"Truly your friend and classmate," Cadet Alexander H. Smith, c. 1870

"Occupants of Room 48, 2nd Stoop, 1872–73"

Barracks stoops and Washington Arch, c. 1876–80

Artillery caissons in front of the west wing of Barracks, c. 1876–80. The darkened portion of the facade outlines repairs made following Hunter's raid.

32

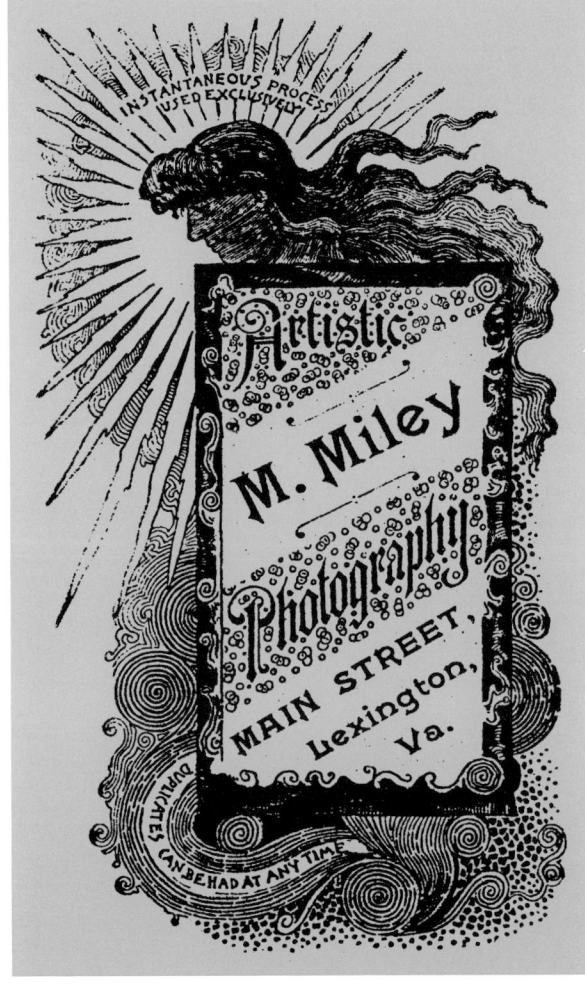

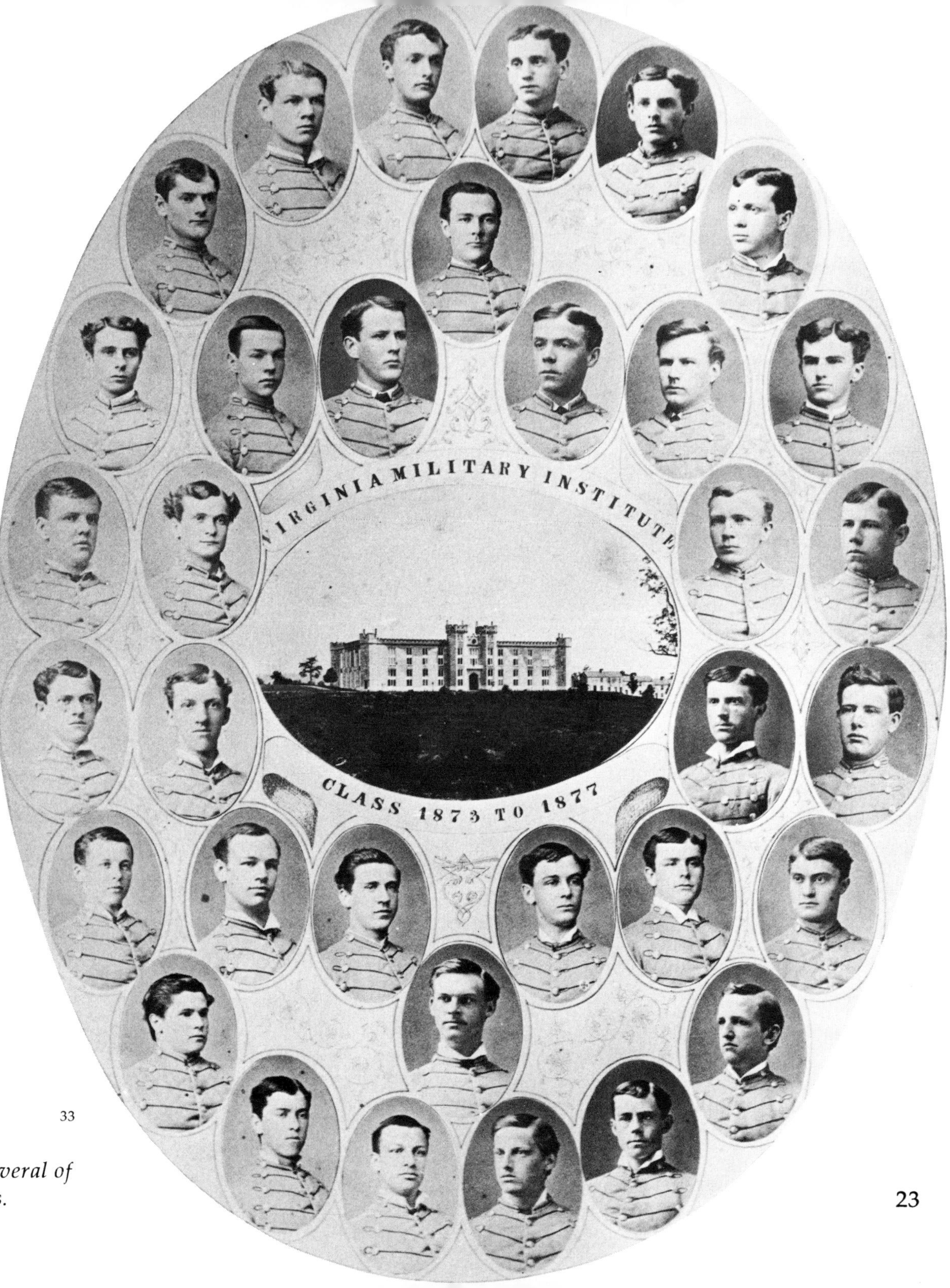

33

The Class of 1877. Michael Miley created several of these composites during the 1870s and 1880s.

34

The Corps at Yorktown, October 20, 1881, for ceremonies marking the 100th anniversary of the British surrender

35

Lexington Gazette, *October 27, 1881*

The Virginia Military Institute Cadets at Yorktown.

CAMP AT YORKTOWN, Oct. 17.

Editors Dispatch:—I came here yesterday morning by the York River route, found conveyances numerous, and paid half a dollar to an old citizen to carry myself, valise, and a basket of provisions to the camp of the Virginia Cadets.

The dust is something fearful. This is no place for ladies or clean clothes.

The Maryland brigade came in fine style yesterday. Their parade was very handsome. Col. H. K. Douglass had a battalion which did well. I did not see the others.

The Virginia Cadets have thus far surpassed all.

The dress-parade yesterday by the corps of Cadets was the very finest I have ever seen.

36

October 18, 1881

GUARD OF HONOR,
(V. M. I. CADETS.)
Yorktown Monument.

LIEUT., G. R. MURRELL.
SERGT. OF GUARD, D. McDONALD.

FIRST RELIEF.
CORPORAL, A. LEE.
PRIVATES.
1 W H. Price, 2 J. M. J. Covey, 3 J. A. McCorkle, 4 L. McC. Gibbs, 5 H. Zuberbier, 6 W. O. Goode, 7 P. Rowe, 8 G. B. Miller.

SECOND RELIEF.
CORPORAL, C. M. SNELLING.
PRIVATES.
1 R. C. Taylor, 2 T. A. Winfield, 3 W. H. Wade, 4 W A Moncure, 5 M. D. Corse, 6 J. G. Breckenridge, 7 G. L. Nicholson, 8 E. Blake.

THIRD RELIEF.
CORPORAL, S. V. FULKERSON.
PRIVATES.
1 G. Baldwin, 2 T. Saunders, 3 A. S. Hightower, 4 L. M. LeHardy, 5 E. Wright, 6 V. L. Terrell, 7 O. Alexander, 8 G. K. Sims.

Parole—EXTRA.
Countersign—DUTY.
YORKTOWN, VA., October 18, 1881.

Compliments of S. V. FULKERSON.

Highlights of the day from the diary of Cadet Thomas J. Nottingham, February–March 1883. The rival "Minks" (Washington College students) are frequently mentioned.

Cadet Thornton Terry (1886–87)

1839. 1889.

Semi-Centennial Celebration
OF THE
Virginia Military Institute.

To all Old Cadets of the Virginia Military Institute, Greeting:

COMRADES,—As Chairman of the Semi-Centennial Executive Committee of the Society of Alumni of the Virginia Military Institute, it is made my pleasant duty to announce that on the **3d and 4th of July proximo** it is proposed by the Alumni to unite in a celebration at the Virginia Military Institute that shall fittingly commemorate the **Semi-Centennial Anniversary** of our cherished **Alma Mater.** It is therefore earnestly hoped that every matriculate now living will strenuously endeavor to lend his presence to the interesting occasion, and participate in the jubilee that, it is believed, will mark a memorable epoch in the history of an institution famous both in war and in peace.

For half a century, amid such vicissitudes as rarely befall an institution of learning, the Virginia Military Institute has unfalteringly prosecuted her glorious mission.

39

"For half a century, amid such vicissitudes as rarely befall an institution of learning, the Virginia Military Institute has unfalteringly prosecuted her glorious mission." Semi-Centennial announcement, 1889.

Alumni gathered in front of the commandant's residence for VMI's Semi-Centennial Celebration, July 4, 1889

41

42

The Semi-Centennial graduating class (1889). This was the last class to graduate before Superintendent Smith retired in December 1889, after fifty years in office. He died on March 21, 1890.

"Rats" with cigarettes, 1890

44

"As Alumni we wish to renew to you the assurances of our most distinguished consideration" (1890s).

45

Advertisement from The Cadet, *a student literary magazine, April 1891*

"The Crowd that took dinner with Miss Freeland and Miss Poor" (1891)

The Class of 1892, wearing mourning bands in memory of fellow cadet Nicholas T. Ingate (November 1889)

48

Roommates William P. Upshur and Joseph C. Allen at home in Barracks, c. 1902

The occupants of No. 92 request the pleasure of your company, in their apartments, on Sunday, December the twenty-fourth, at half-past five o'clock.

49

1899

50

The Corps marching in William Howard Taft's inaugural parade, March 4, 1909

Cadets Left This Morning for Washington

The cadets of the Virginia Military Institute, three hundred strong and headed by the post band, marched from barracks to the union station this morning and left Lexington at 7 o'clock on a special train of seven coaches for Washington to participate tomorrow in the parade incident to the inauguration of President Taft. The trip is to be made over the Chesapeake and Ohio railroad by Bremo and Gordonsville, and they expect to reach the capital city at 2 o'clock this afternoon. At Gordonsville the Stonewall band of Staunton will join the Institute band and will accompany the latter in the parade.

The cadets are under command of Colonel M. M. Mills, the commandant. A dress parade and drill by the cadets is scheduled for this afternoon on the White House grounds and later at the War Department building is to take place a flag presentation. The New York alumni of the V. M. I. have arranged for the presentation to the battalion a facsimile of the flag carried by the V. M. I. boys in the New Market battle during the Civil War. The presentation is to be made by Secretary of War Wright, and Governor Swanson is expected to receive the flag on behalf of the cadets.

51

Lexington Gazette, March 3, 1909

"Airing the Hay"—bedclothes on stoops, c. 1903

Reveille to Taps

TIME has left the daily life of a cadet essentially unaltered. Some regulations have changed, but cadets from the 1840s to the present have responded to the call of reveille in the morning and to the sound of taps at night. This continuity is illustrated by a letter from Cadet Edward Minor Watson to his "Pa." Writing on September 17, 1868, Cadet Watson describes a daily routine that would sound familiar to every VMI alumnus. In this chapter, excerpts from Watson's letter serve as companion pieces for photographs depicting the academic and military aspects of cadet life.

16   Virginia Military Institute.

Use of tobacco.   72. No Cadet shall in any way use tobacco, nor bring it or cause it to be brought into either barracks or camp, nor have it in his room, or otherwise in his possession.

Cooking.   73. No Cadet shall cook or prepare food in either barracks or in camp, nor give an entertainment there or elsewhere without permission.

Keeping horse, &c.   74. No Cadet shall be allowed to keep a waiter, horse or dog.

Damage to quarters.   75. Any Cadet who shall wantonly damage any quarters, or their appurtenances, shall, besides making good such damages, be otherwise punished, according to the nature of his offence.

53

From Regulations of the Virginia Military Institute at Lexington *(1839)*

"At 5 o'clock . . . I [was] awakened by a most dreadful noise. I at first thought that the house was falling or that a volcano had burst in about a quarter of a mile from I hardly knew where, as I found myself lying with nothing between me and floor except a mattress about three feet wide. I was soon enlightened as to the cause of the disturbence, by an old cadet, who in the dim light of the *very* early morning, as he stood dressing close by I had not noticed. He remarked in a tone which seemed anything but motherly, 'Rat get *UP* Sir, and go to revilee.' At this I opened my eyes somewhat wider, and remembering the state of affairs I thought it best to do as he said."

Cadet Edward M. Watson to "Pa," September 17, 1868

54

Late for roll call, c. 1890. The bugle replaced the fife and drum in 1906.

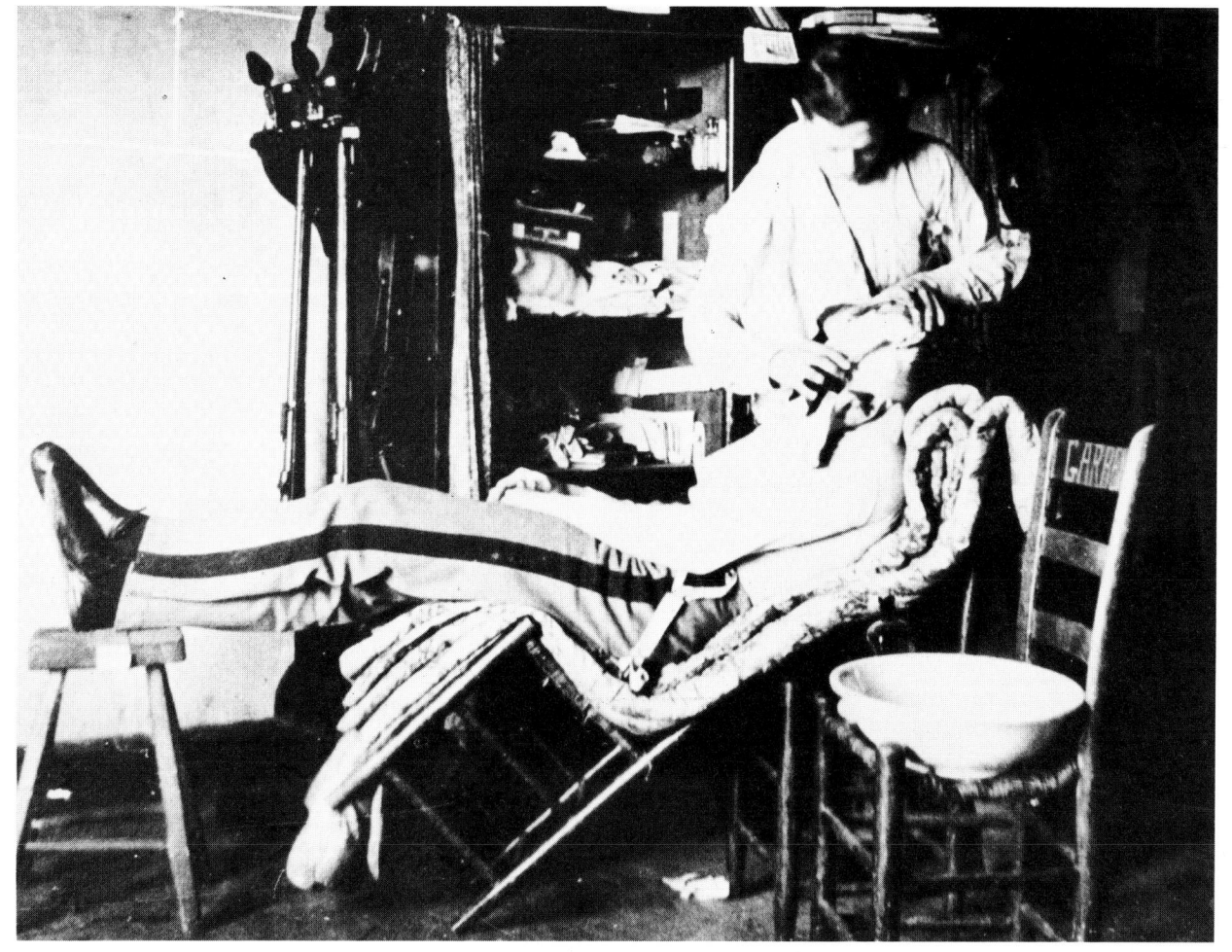

Getting a shave, c. 1905

"We were then disbanded and were given ½ hour to make our toilets and clean up our room. In cleaning up our room we have to take everything from the tables and chairs and put them in their proper place and have to roll up our beds in a bundle.... At the end of the half hour the inspector visits."

Cadet Edward M. Watson to "Pa," September 17, 1868

"Where whiskers are worn, they must not extend below the line drawn from the tip of the ear to the corner of the mouth." Superintendent's order specifying length of hair, June 1, 1844

57

Laundry detail, 1904–5

"A corner of a V.M.I. boudoir" (c. 1900)

Rat "finned out" (1904–5). New cadets were required to assume this position at the command of upperclassmen.

"**The drum calls us to study.** We recite until one o'clock when time is given for dinner.... At 2 o'clock we are again called to study. At 4 o'clock we are dismissed."

Cadet Edward M. Watson to "Pa," September 17, 1868

61

Cadets marching to the Francis H. Smith Academic Building, c. 1902. This classroom building was opened in 1900 and demolished in 1923 to provide space for the north wing of Barracks. An electric clock was added to the tower soon after construction was completed.

From Register of the Officers and Cadets, *July 1855. This list reflects the increase in faculty and academic specialties during the 1840s and 1850s. Noteworthy among those joining the academic staff before the Civil War were Thomas H. Williamson (1841), William Gilham (1846), Robert Emmet Rodes (1848), and Thomas J. Jackson (1851).*

ACADEMIC STAFF.

Col. Francis H. Smith, A. M., Superintendent and Professor of Mathematics.

Capt. J. G. Gamble, Assistant Professor of Mathematics, and Assistant Instructor of Tactics.

Cadet S. Crutchfield, (First Class) Acting Assistant Professor of Mathematics.

Major J. T. L. Preston, A. M., Professor of Languages and English Literature.

Lieut. G. H. Smith, Assistant Professor of Languages, and Assistant Instructor in Infantry Tactics.

Cadet L. T. W. Patton, (First Class,) Acting Assistant Professor of Languages.

Major T. H. Williamson, Professor of Engineering and Instructor of Drawing.

Major William Gilham, A. M., Professor of Chemistry, and Instructor of Infantry Tactics and Commandant of Cadets.

Major Thomas J. Jackson, Professor of Natural and Experimental Philosophy and Instructor of Artillery.

Major R. E. Colston, Professor of French Language.

MILITARY STAFF.

H. M. Estill, M. D.,	Surgeon.
R. E. Colston,	Treasurer.
Lieut. G. H. Smith,	Adjutant.
R. H. Catlett,	Quarter Master.
J. T. Gibbs,	Commissary and Steward.

"Look there stands Jackson like a mud wall" (1877). Satirizing VMI's traditions and pointing out the foibles of their professors were favorite pastimes of cadets, as seen in many nineteenth-century drawings, diaries, letters, and in this detail from a class cartoon.

64

From Register of Officers
and Cadets, *July 1855*

65

Thomas Hoomes Williamson, c. 1875. Williamson (1813–1888) was a distinguished engineer, architect, and educator who developed VMI's engineering curriculum during his forty-seven years on the faculty.

Architectural drawing by Cadet Edward L. Smith (1854), one of a series of drawings required of cadets taking Professor Williamson's courses

67

A view from the Parade Ground, c. 1889, showing the Superintendent's Quarters (center, constructed 1860) and the Gilham residence (right, constructed 1852). Both residences were designed by Alexander Jackson Davis, a nationally prominent architect noted for his work in the Gothic style. Davis also designed Barracks and other major buildings at VMI.

68

The front (Washington Arch facade) of Barracks, c. 1889. A. J. Davis submitted his plan for this facade in 1850, and construction began the same year.

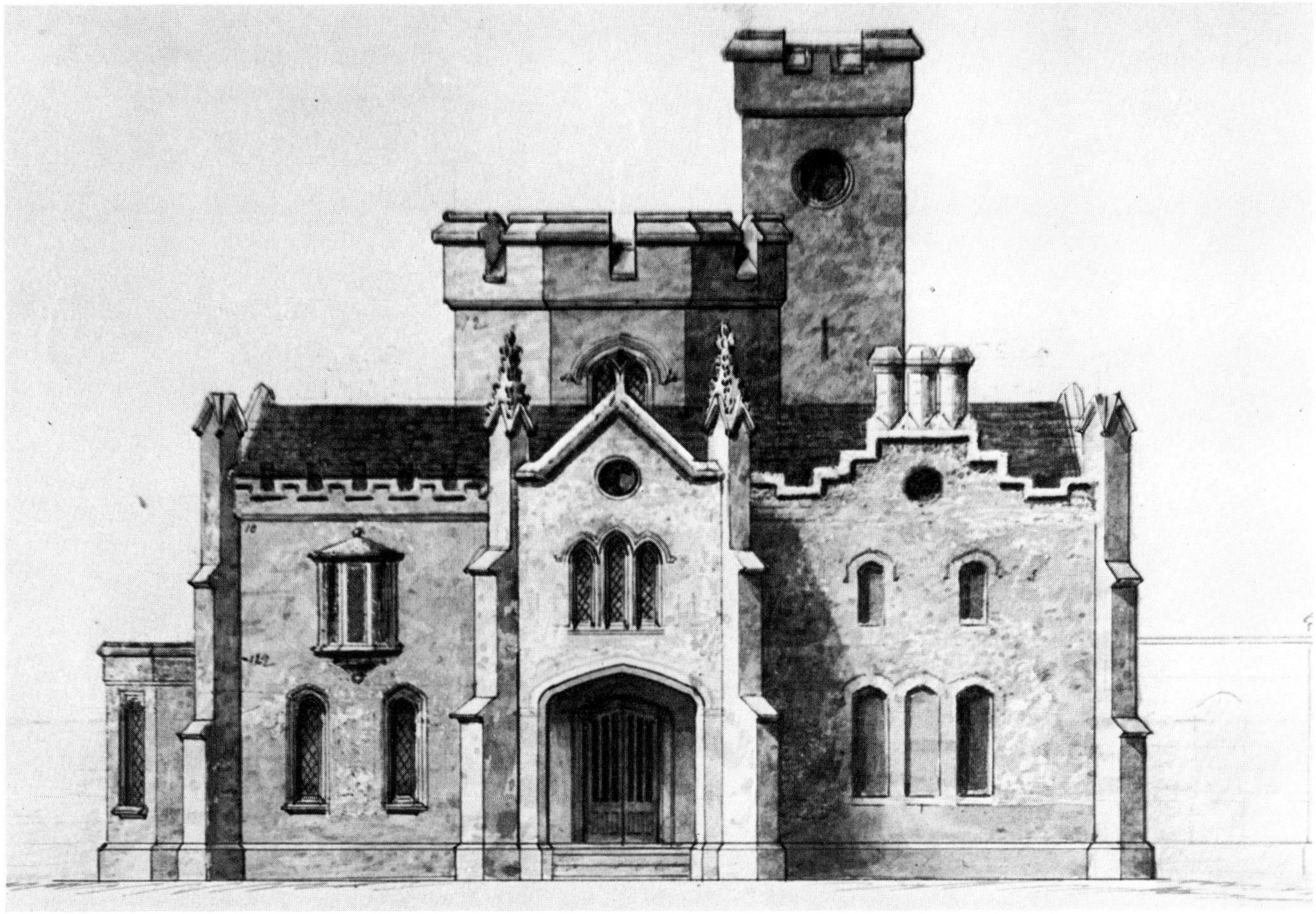

69

Early plan for the Williamson residence by A. J. Davis (c. 1850). This residence, later known as the Commandant's Quarters, had an eventful life before it was razed in 1964: it was destroyed in Hunter's raid, rebuilt in 1865–66, and moved in 1915.

70

"Received of Col. F. H. Smith the sum of two hundred dollars, being in full for designs, drawings, details &c for Barracks, Professors' Houses &c at Lexington, Va. to this date. Alex. J. Davis." From Treasurer's Records, 1851

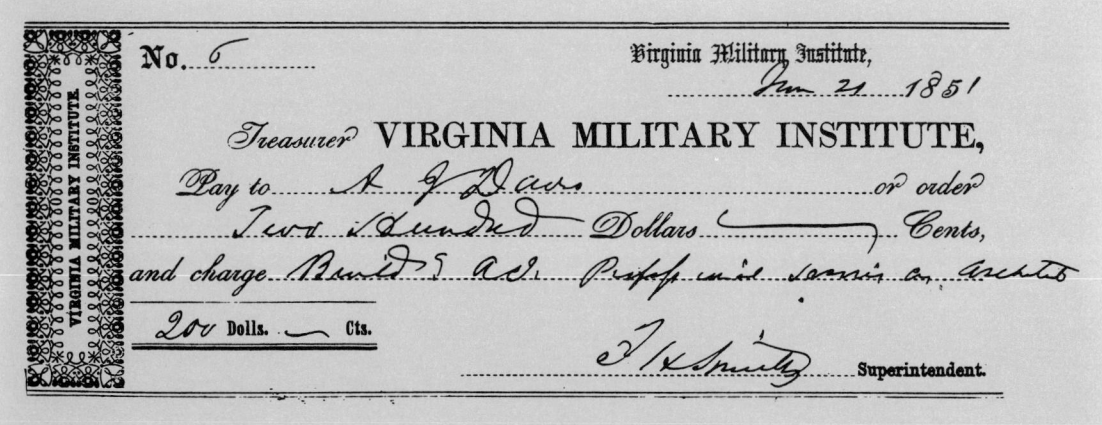

"Gen. Custis Lee has consented to serve.... The greatest piece of news is, that Washington College has prevailed upon Gen. R. E. Lee to take the Pres. of the College.... While I will say to you that high is my admiration of the father as a General & gentleman—the son is the better man for the Professorship."

Francis H. Smith to Scott Shipp, September 1, 1865

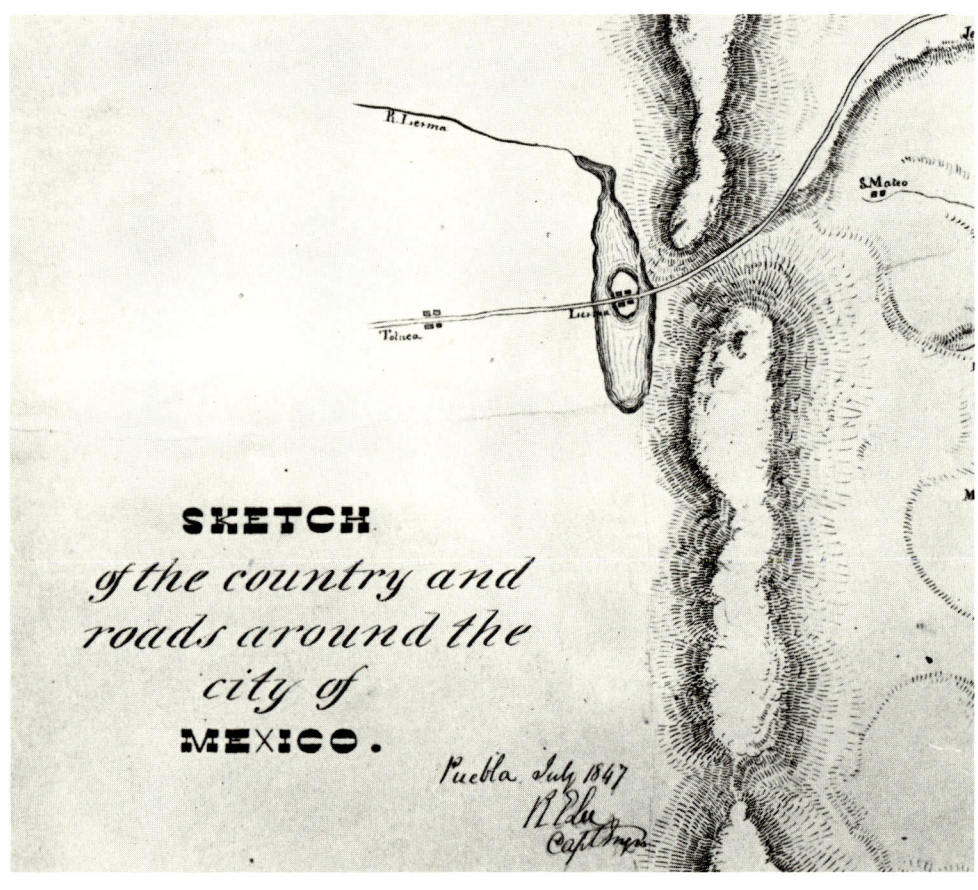

G. W. Custis Lee, c. 1866. Lee joined VMI's faculty in 1865 as professor of civil and military engineering and applied mechanics. When General Robert E. Lee died in 1870, Custis Lee left the Institute in order to succeed his father as president of Washington College.

Detail from "Sketch of the country and roads around the city of Mexico," July 1847. Part of a collection of thirty maps used by Robert E. Lee in the Mexican War and given to VMI by G. W. C. Lee in 1898

Classroom scene, 1899

John Mercer Brooke, c. 1867. On October 9, 1865, the Board of Visitors created "a Professorship of Practical Astronomy, Geodesy, Physical Geography and Meteorology." Brooke, an 1847 Naval Academy graduate who contributed to the design of the **Merrimack** *and invented the "Brooke Gun," was appointed to the new position.*

74

75

Matthew Fontaine Maury in academic robes donned for his acceptance of an honorary degree from Cambridge University (1868). Maury, a noted oceanographer and physical scientist, came to VMI in the fall of 1868. He became Brooke's colleague in the newly established Department of Physics and was placed in charge of conducting a physical survey of Virginia. Maury's geography books were standard texts at VMI and many other colleges.

76

Quarterly Grade Report of Cadet Joseph H. Chenoweth, July 10, 1856

77

Faculty, 1878–79. In the center is Superintendent Smith; clockwise from top center are: Scott Shipp, Thomas H. Williamson, Marshall McDonald, Robert L. Madison, Mark B. Hardin, James H. Morrison, William M. Patton, John W. Lyell, Thomas M. Semmes, and John M. Brooke.

Engineering and drawing professor Robert A. Marr in his classroom, c. 1895

79

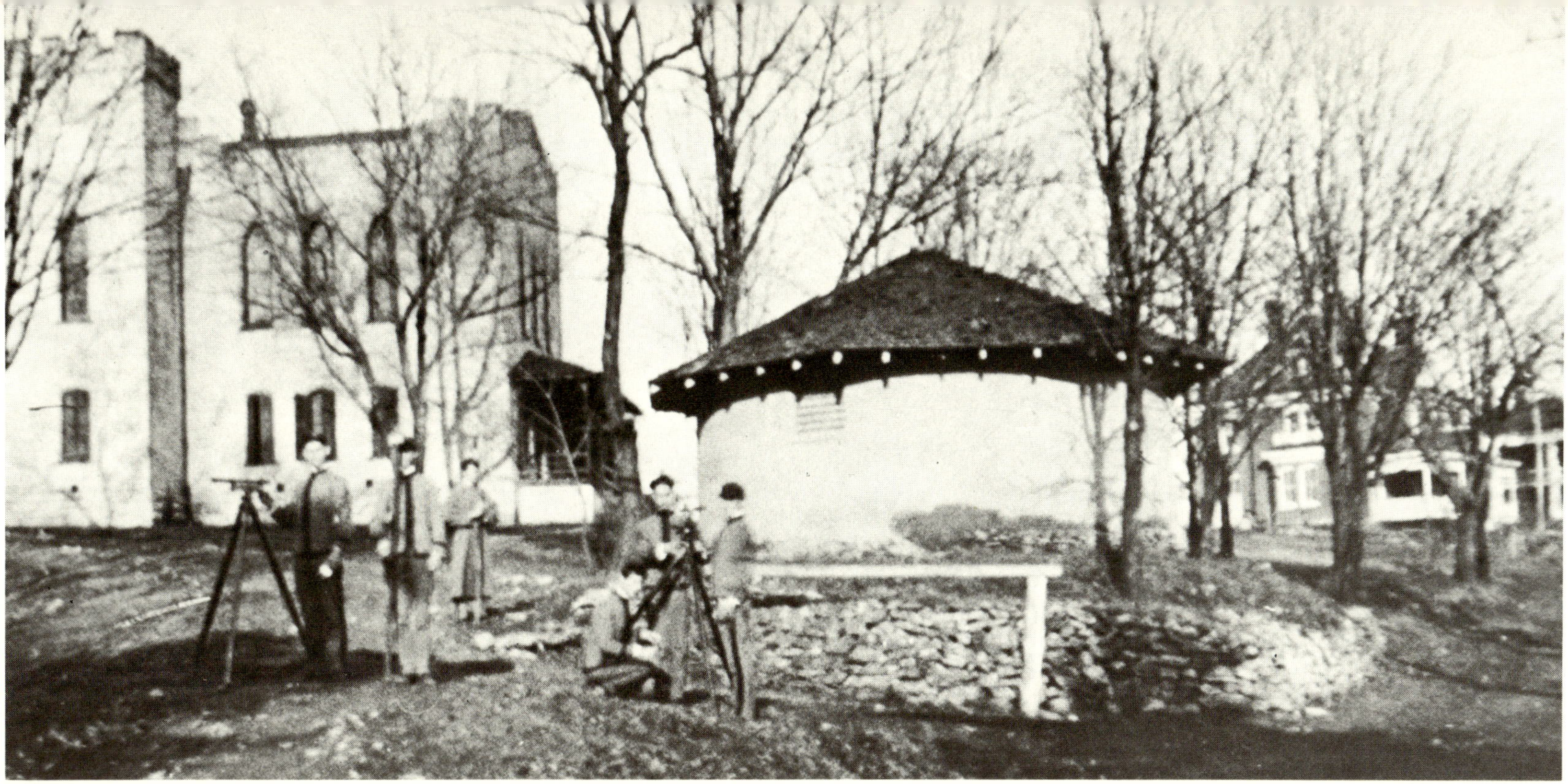

Members of a surveying class at work near the old Mess Hall and Ice House, c. 1903

80

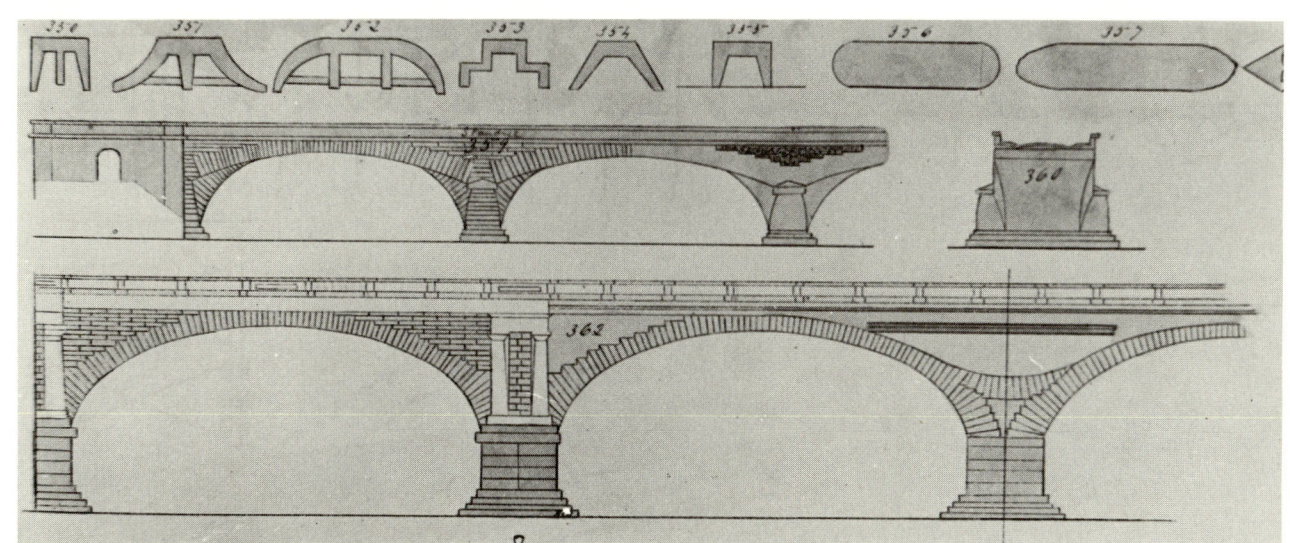

Detail from an engineering drawing by Cadet Edward C. Shepherd (1853)

81
Superintendent Francis H. Smith shortly before his retirement (c. 1889)

82
Advertisement promoting Smith's mathematics texts (1855)

83

Clock tower on Smith Academic Building, 1904–5

84

Group in front of old Jackson Memorial Hall, c. 1900. This extension of the west wing of Barracks, built in 1896, housed the Engineering Department and the Drawing Academy and provided space for dances and many other activities. Jackson Arch was spared when the Hall was demolished in 1916 to make room for more cadet quarters.

Superintendent Scott Shipp (center, front row) and faculty, 1892–93. Mathematics professor Edward West Nichols (seated at far left) graduated from VMI in 1878 and became the Institute's third superintendent in 1907.

Artillery drill, c. 1903

Saber drill on Parade Ground, c. 1903

> "**At 4½ we are called for evening drills.** The drill lasts 1½ hours. We have then 15 minutes to fix for dress parade. After parade 5 minutes is given to change clothes."
>
> *Cadet Edward M. Watson to "Pa," September 17, 1868*

The Corps of Cadets at stacked arms, c. 1893

Guard mount with band, c. 1895

"With a view to the early resumption of Infantry Drill, Captains will divide their companies into squads, and assign drill masters. Those cadets reckoned as the best soldiers must not be grouped in squads, but distributed equally throughout the Company. In no case will a squad be composed wholly of awkward men."

Order concerning infantry drill, March 22, 1870

Band member John Illig, c. 1890. The VMI Band consisted of civilian musicians until 1947, when the first cadet band was established.

Camp scene, c. 1868–72. The first summer camp was established in July 1840, on the Institute's Parade Ground. Except for those who were granted a summer furlough, all cadets lived in camp after the First Class graduated in July until the beginning of the academic year in September. "Rats" arrived sometime during the encampment, and the camp order books contain many references to demerits given to old cadets who engaged in hazing the newcomers. Toward the end of the summer, the Corps frequently tried out their camping skills in the field by going on a "practice march" to Rockbridge Alum Springs or other local spots. Camp remained a fixture of cadet life throughout the nineteenth century, although the time and place of encampment changed.

"The musicians failed to beat reveille." Guard report from Camp Gregory, August 8, 1842

> "**We then march to supper.** ... Each one having reached the seat assigned assumes the position of a soldier and standing staring [at] the boy on the opposite of the table in the face (who by the way in my case is mighty ugly). We have to wait until every body has found his place. Then at the word 'be seated' each head of the three hundred cadets bobs down and we commence eating."

Cadet Edward M. Watson to "Pa." September 17, 1868

In the Mess Hall, c. 1903

94

The old Mess Hall (c. 1876–80), designed by A. J. Davis, was built in 1854 and was destroyed by fire in 1905.

"Growley"

'Twas at the ancient V. M. I.,
    At mess in Company A.,
When first I saw the growley dish,
    And fainted dead away.

As you will ask what "Growley" means,
    To you I will explain—
Although when I recall the truck,
    It fills my soul with pain.

Of all the hash I ever saw,
    This dish it takes the cake;
Give me my choice fair youthful " cit
    I'd much prefer a snake.

But what a soldier has for food,
    At this old V. M. I.,
Would make an Anaconda sick—
    A Hottentot would die.

95

From The Bomb, cadet yearbook, 1895

"Today for breakfast we had only two pieces of bread and about a half gill of milk with what we call growly which is made of mutton beef beef feet or any other thing they can make for dinner. We have beef and cabbage or turnips one day and beef steak and soup the next. We have nothing that I would have eaten at home but I am so hungry when I go to meals that I think even turnips delicious, but I live off of it very well.... Every one says I have fattened very much."

Cadet Edmund Berkeley to his mother, November 26, 1863

Cook Patrick Payne, c. 1890

> Resolved, That the following bill of fare be submitted to the applicants for the place of Steward, and that they be required to submit sealed proposals for the boarding of the Cadets according to the s'd bill. Viz
> For Breakfast
> Hot Corn Cakes, & fresh light bread
> Butter, Coffee & Cold meat.
> Dinner
> Two varieties of Meat, two kinds of Vegetables.
> Cold light bread, or, Corn bread.
> Supper
> Same as breakfast — exchanging Coffee, for tea, or milk occasionally.
> Plain desert once a week. When a Cadet is sick, he shall have such fare, as the Surgeon shall prescribe, and receive proper and necessary attention from the Steward.
> Ordered that the Board be adjourned until Monday Morning at 8 O'clock.

The Mess Hall's first bill of fare was adopted by the Board of Visitors on May 31, 1839.

98

The VMI Library, located in Barracks, as it was in the 1890s. The library has had many homes since it was established in 1840. Early locations included the Mess Hall and the Gun Shed. Although Hunter's troops destroyed most of the Institute's books in 1864, the library was reestablished in 1868 in the west wing of Barracks. It remained there until 1907, when a new library building was constructed.

> "**We have then 15 minutes, when we are called to study.** We study untill half past nine when we are called to tattoo. Then in five minutes the drum sounds for blowing out lights."

Cadet Edward M. Watson to "Pa," September 17, 1868

Exterior of the 1907 Library (c. 1910). This photograph also shows **Virginia Mourning Her Dead** *in its original location in front of old Jackson Memorial Hall.*

Interior of the 1907 Library (c. 1910). Although a more spacious library, named for J. T. L. Preston, was dedicated in 1939, the 1907 building was not torn down until the late 1940s.

> "The Inspector visits immediately to see that every body is in bed and then nothing is heard but the tread or challenge of the sentinel untill five in the morning."

Cadet Edward M. Watson to "Pa," September 17, 1868

Members of the Guard, c. 1890. White pith helmets were part of the summer uniform for a brief period during the 1890s.

Guard report, January 17, 1884. Prisoners were charged with "throwing explosive articles on stoop."

> "I can assure you that I am heartily sick of the Military, studies & everything else connected with the V.M.I. & I don't think I will touch a gun, book, or anything that bears any resemblance to them for some time after I leave here, that is if I ever do get away."

Cadet Charles M. Barton to his cousin Joe, September 28, 1855

"Homesick" (c. 1905)

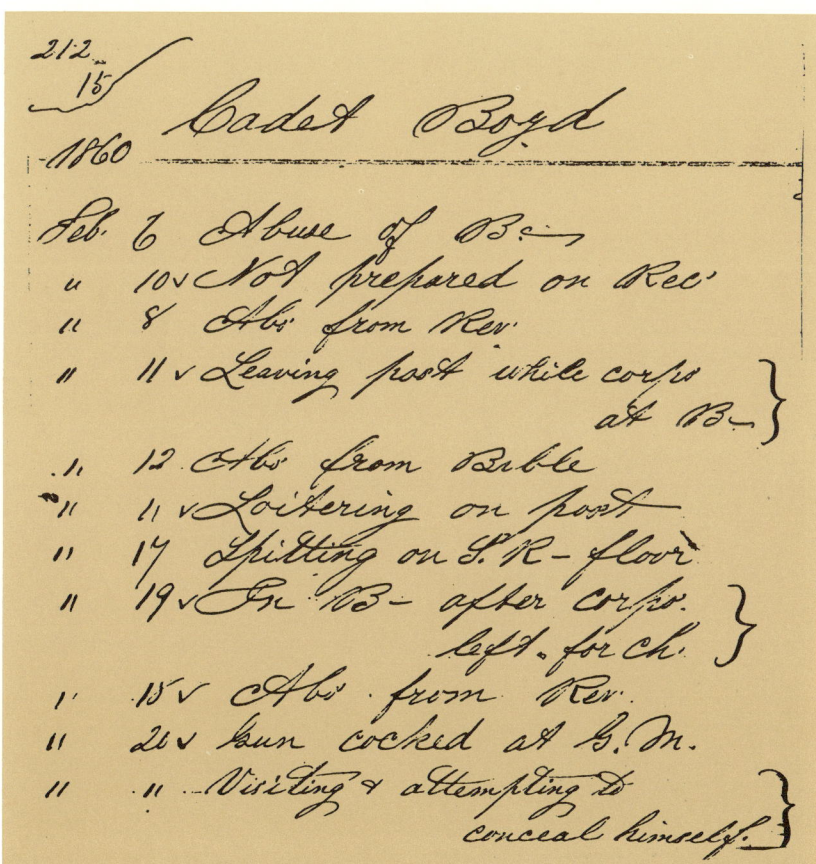

Entry from Demerit Book, 1860. Cadet Boyd's sins included "visiting and attempting to conceal himself."

Team Spirit,

Gymnasium team performing stunt, c. 1898

Calics, and "Frolics after Taps"

THE drudgery of study and drill seems endless, but a cadet can always look forward to life's finer pleasures. There are games to play, pretty young ladies to escort, and, of course, the joy of successfully circumventing the regulations.

From The Bomb, *1908*

"Yesterday one of my roommates (as it was his time) went out in the country *foraging* and about 12 o'clock he came in with two very nice *chickens* with their heads looking like some one had hit them with a rock; well I was not with Morgan but I guess the chickens tried to *hurt him* and he had to hit them in *self defence*; anyhow we had a very nice breakfast this morning in old 45 (no. of our room) of fried chicken, butter and warm biscuits which I assure you was not at all objectionable, and I think from experience that the old saying is true that '*stolen* things always eat the sweetest.'"

Cadet Samuel F. Atwill to his mother, September 28, 1862

Football team, 1889-90

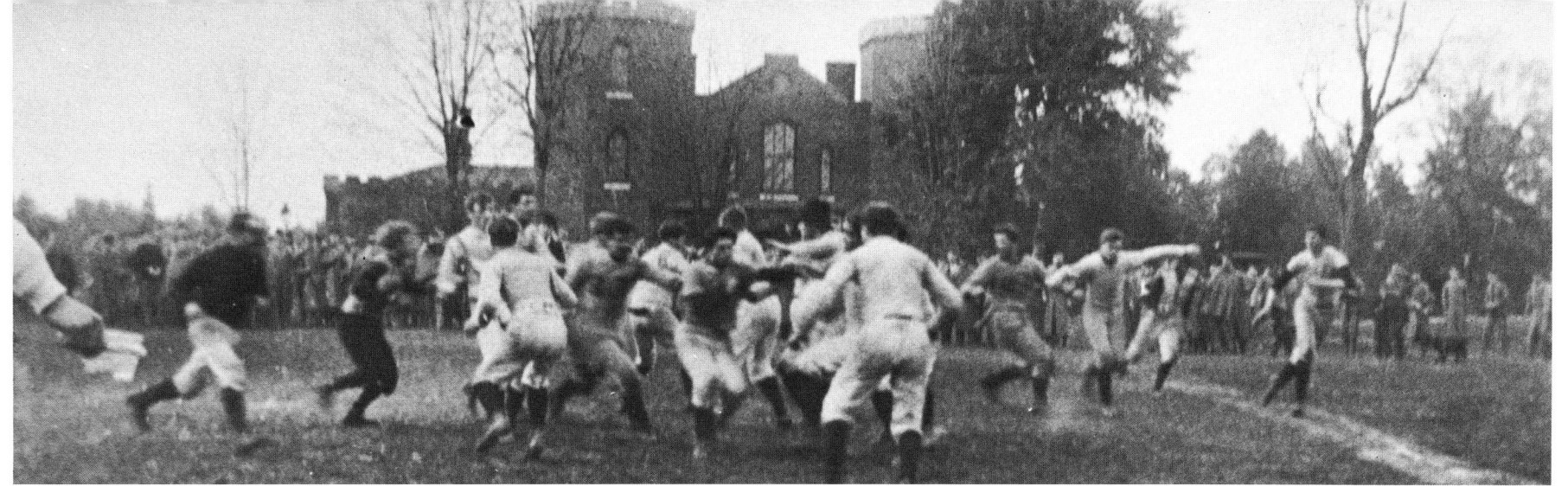

108

VMI vs. St. John's College, c. 1892

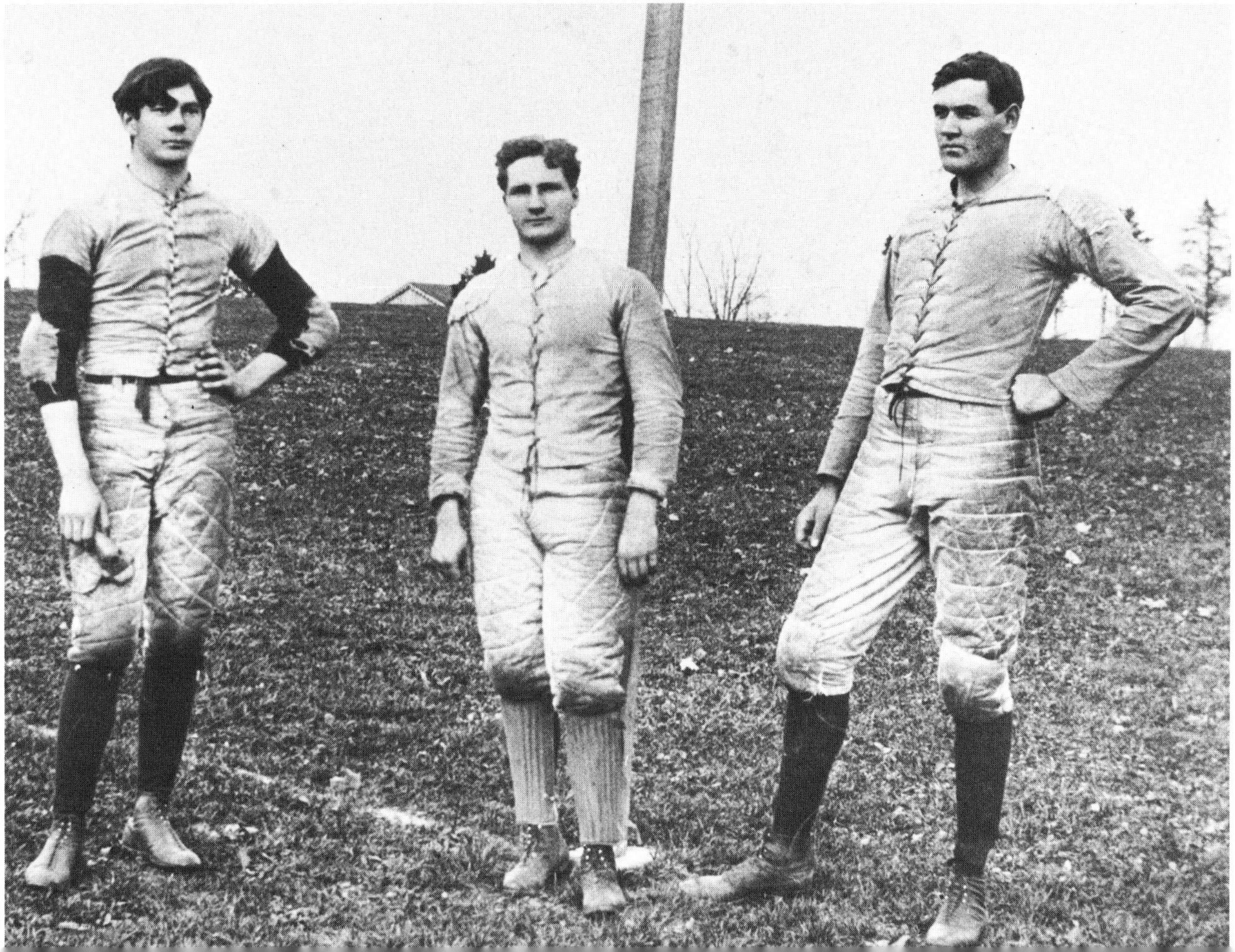

1893

October	14.	W. L. U.,	0	V. M. I.,	28
"	21.	U. N. C.,	4	"	10
November	11.	Richmond College,	0	"	34
"	25.	U. Va.,	22	"	0

1892

October	27.	St. Johns,	0	V. M. I.,	18
November	11.	Wake Forest,	12	"	12
"	19.	Trinity,	0	"	34
"	29.	State College, Ky.,	0	"	34
———	.	W. L. U.,	6	"	30

110

From The Bomb, *1895*

109

Three football players (1893). Left to right: *Richard N. Poindexter, Douglas H. Smith, Harry E. Biscoe*

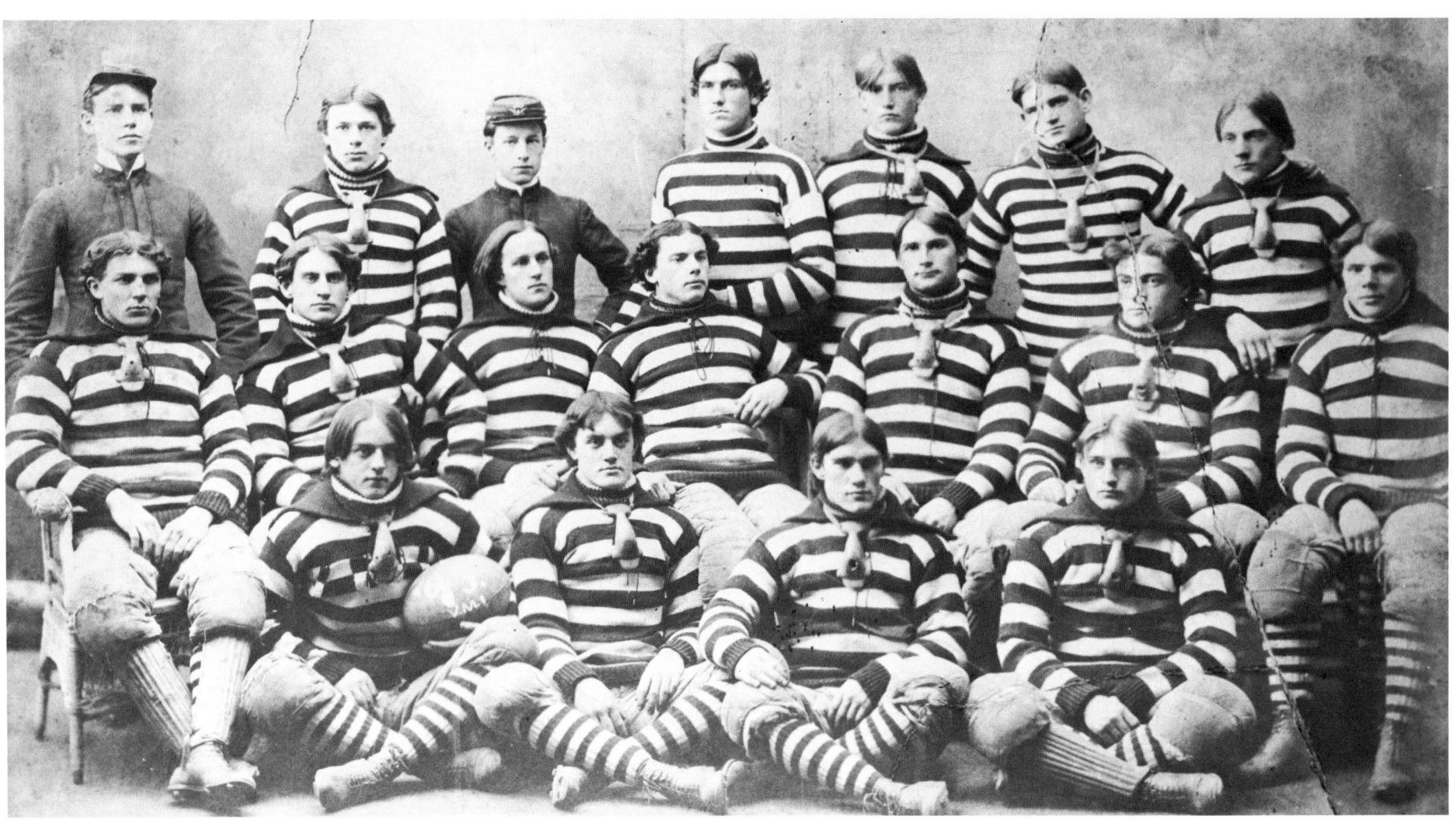

111

Football team, 1895

The Red, White, and Yellow floats on high,
The Institute shall never die,
So now "keydets" with one voice cry—
God bless our team and V.M.I.   Amen.

VMI Doxology, 1903

112

Detail from team photograph, 1900. Left tackle George C. Marshall (lower right) graduated in 1901 and went on to become the Institute's most distinguished alumnus. Marshall served as chief of staff of the army during World War II, as secretary of state and secretary of defense, and was awarded the Nobel Prize for Peace in 1953.

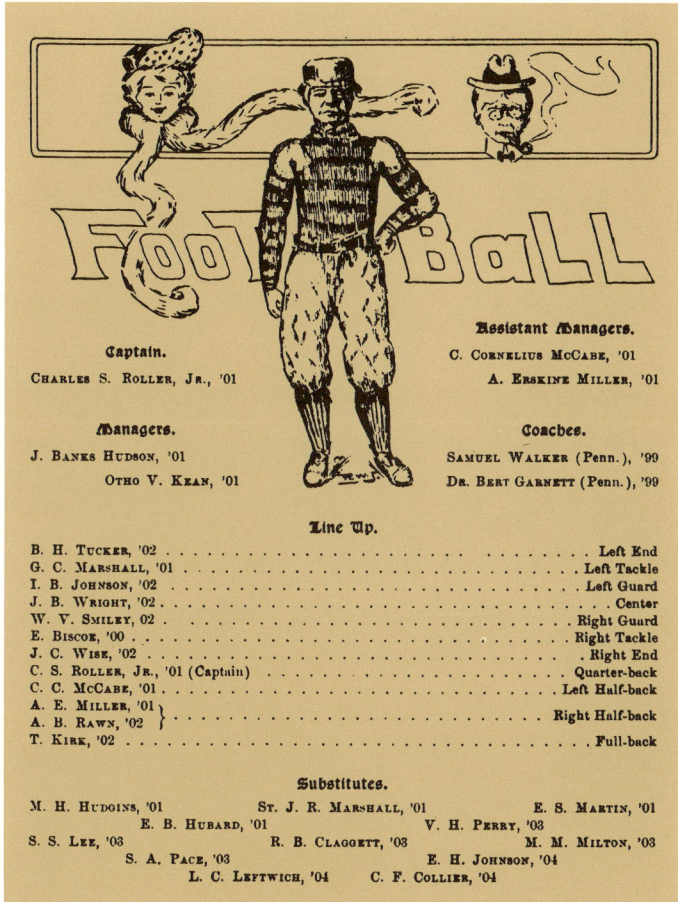

113

From The Bomb, *1901*

114

Baseball team, 1897

2 — 22	
V. M. I. vs. W. & L.,	
Tuesday, May 1, 1900.	

115

BASS BALL.—A match game between the Second nine of the College Club and the first nine of the Pelha Club of the Institute was played on Saturday evening, and resulted in a victory to the Cadets, after a spirited and very close contest.

116

Lexington Gazette, May 12, 1869

11 — 9
V. M. I. vs. Roanoke College,
Saturday, April 14, 1900.

117

BASE-BALL!
W. & L. VS. V. M. I.

Crawford + Guion, Booker   Carneal + Raller

Saturday, April 7, 1900.
UNIVERSITY GROUNDS.

Game Called at 3:15 P. M.

Admission 50c.   Boys 25c.   Ladies Free.

Pitcher Albert B. DeVault, c. 1908

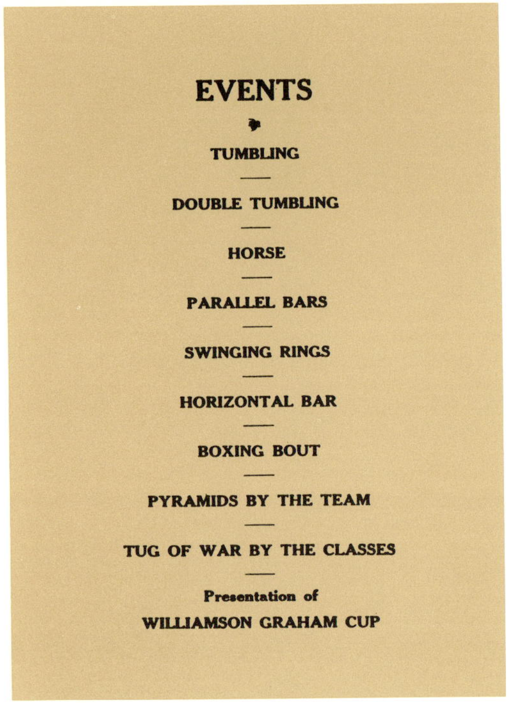

EVENTS

TUMBLING

DOUBLE TUMBLING

HORSE

PARALLEL BARS

SWINGING RINGS

HORIZONTAL BAR

BOXING BOUT

PYRAMIDS BY THE TEAM

TUG OF WAR BY THE CLASSES

Presentation of
WILLIAMSON GRAHAM CUP

1910

"VMI Gymnasium Club. Best Athletic Performance ever given, June 21, 1887. James M. Redfield, Simon K. Owens, Samuel D. Rockenbach, Robert C. George, Nathaniel B. Tucker."

Tennis club, 1895

VMI's first intercollegiate basketball team. From The Bomb, *1909*

124

Ice hockey on the North (now Maury) River, 1904–5

125

Order granting permission to go skating, February 2, 1886

126

Sleigh ride, c. 1900

127

Snow scene, c. 1903

"The day being very muddy and sloppy there was an unusual display of *legs* by the young ladies of the Seminary."

From diary of Cadet Charles T. Haigh, March 27, 1863

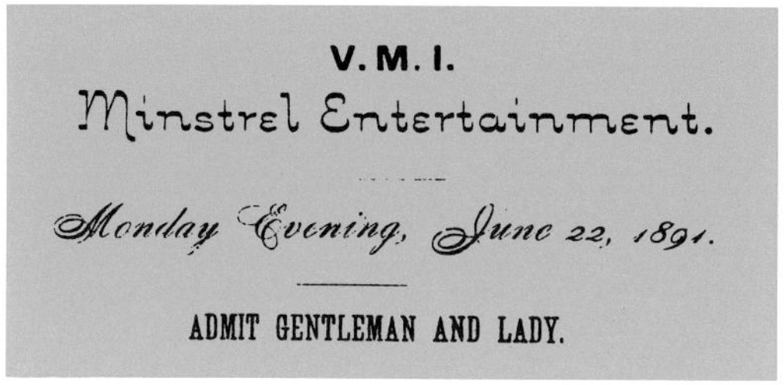
V. M. I.

Minstrel Entertainment.

Monday Evening, June 22, 1891.

ADMIT GENTLEMAN AND LADY.

128

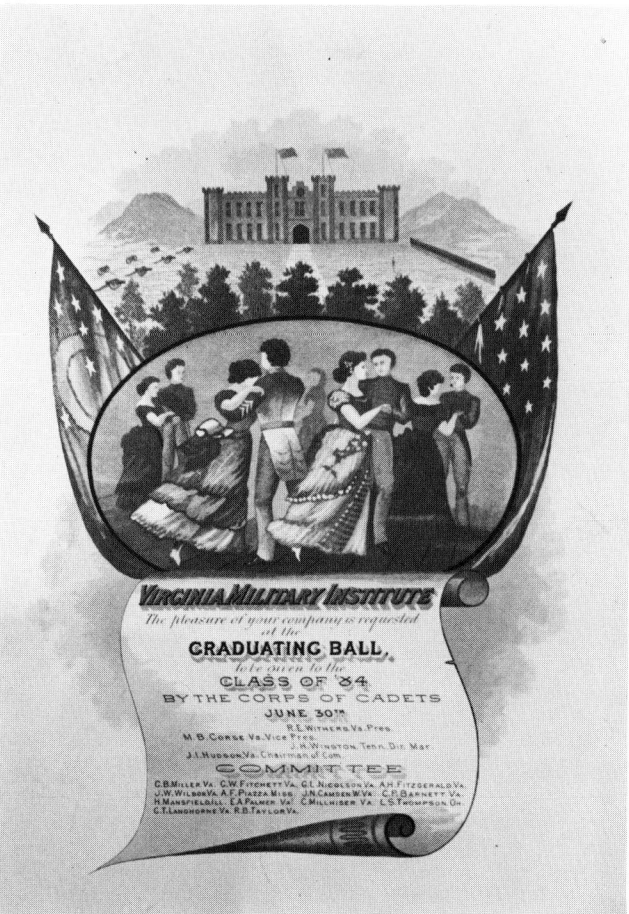

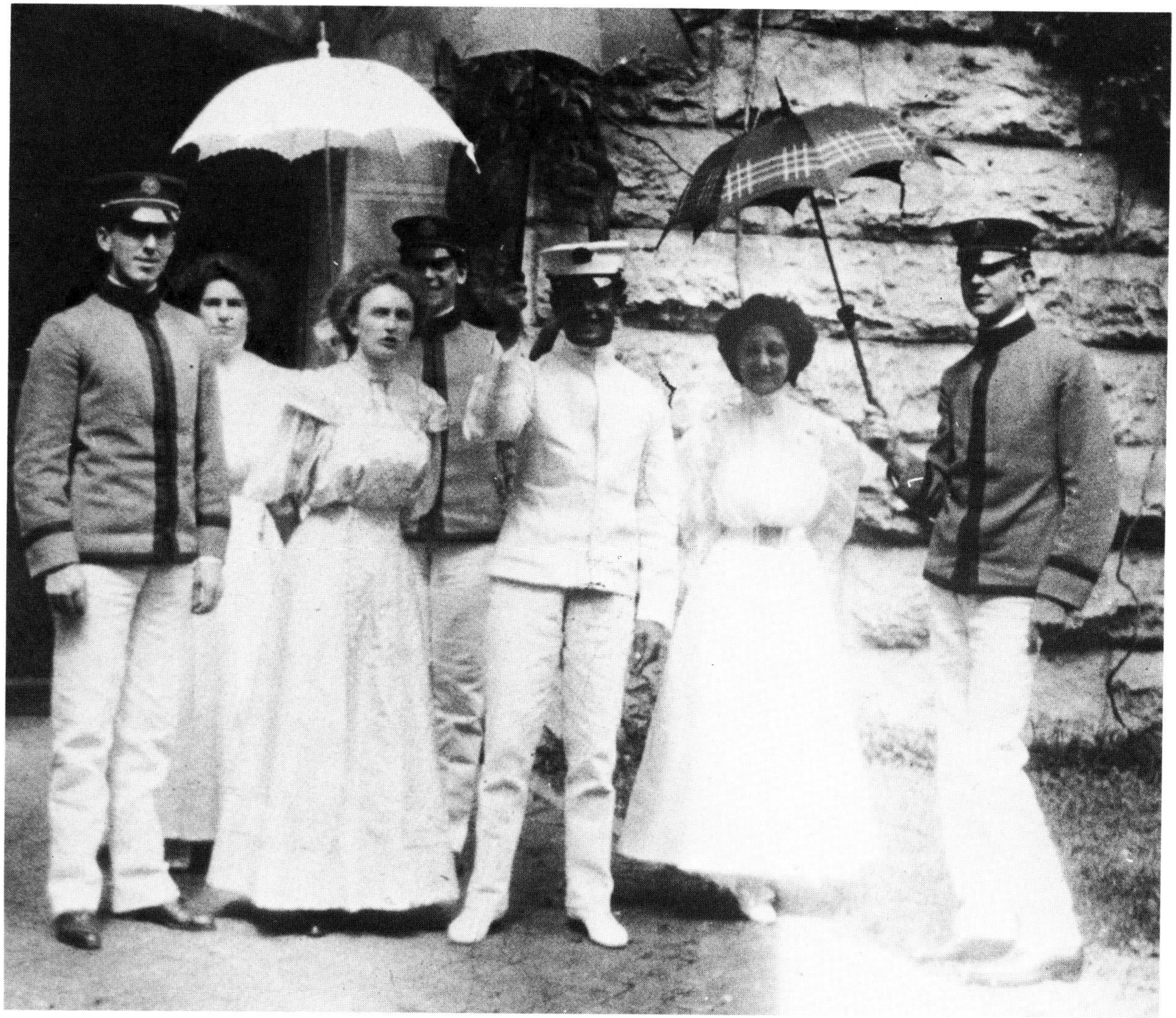

129

Spring outing, c. 1908

130

"The changing of the Guard" (c. 1890)

" 'Art. 23rd of the Regulations' says 'if any cadet shall be married while at the Institute, such marriage will be considered as equivalent to a resignation, and he will leave then.' As I expect to be married in the course of four or five weeks I have felt it to be my duty to give you timely intimation of the fact & tender you my resignation."

Cadet Walter Bowen to Superintendent Smith, August 17, 1842

THE CADETS' BALL.

The annual Ball of the Corps of Cadets which came off on the evening of the 3rd, was truly a brilliant affair. We do not know that we have ever witnessed a more beautiful and fascinating company of ladies than was there assembled. Richmond, Staunton, Lynchburg and Liberty, furnished their full quotas of these light troops, who, we fear, have been most destructive to our young soldiers of the V. M. I. The dancing was kept up until a late hour, the company before dispersing having partaken of a most sumptuous repast prepared by the hospitable steward of the Institute, Mr. W. S. Eskridge. All seemed happy, and no doubt went away wishing many a return of these delightful parties.

132

"A most sumptuous repast."
Lexington Gazette, July 9, 1846

133

Miss Frances Lewis Roller and Miss Margaret Stuart Roller (top row) and friends, c. 1892

134

Skinny-dipping, c. 1908

135

"The cadets will . . . bathe at such places, as may not offend the delicacy of females passing the Bridge at Jordans." Order, June 23, 1858

"The Oyster Supper—A frolic after taps"

Two first classmen from near that immortal city of Norfolk received last Tuesday by Col. Spex & Co.'s express—a box.... I was busy writing a letter ... when all at once ... my letter was chased completely from my mind by a certain *Richard* coming into our room and saying "boys, we have some oysters—hope you will come around after taps."... When taps had beat and Massie's footsteps had died away No. 19 was deserted.... While on our way we heard doors open and shut and footsteps following fast to No. 23. There we found some 20 or 25 fellows all with eager & fascinated eyes gazing on the eatables.... There heaped up on mess hall soup plates reigned *Pickled oysters* triumphant.... In the center of all lay a goodly number of the finest segars.

A recollection of a special night in barracks, by Philip C. Gibbs, Class of 1851

"Two cadets were seen smoking segars in the public streets." Order, August 27, 1842

New Year's Eve (c. 1893)

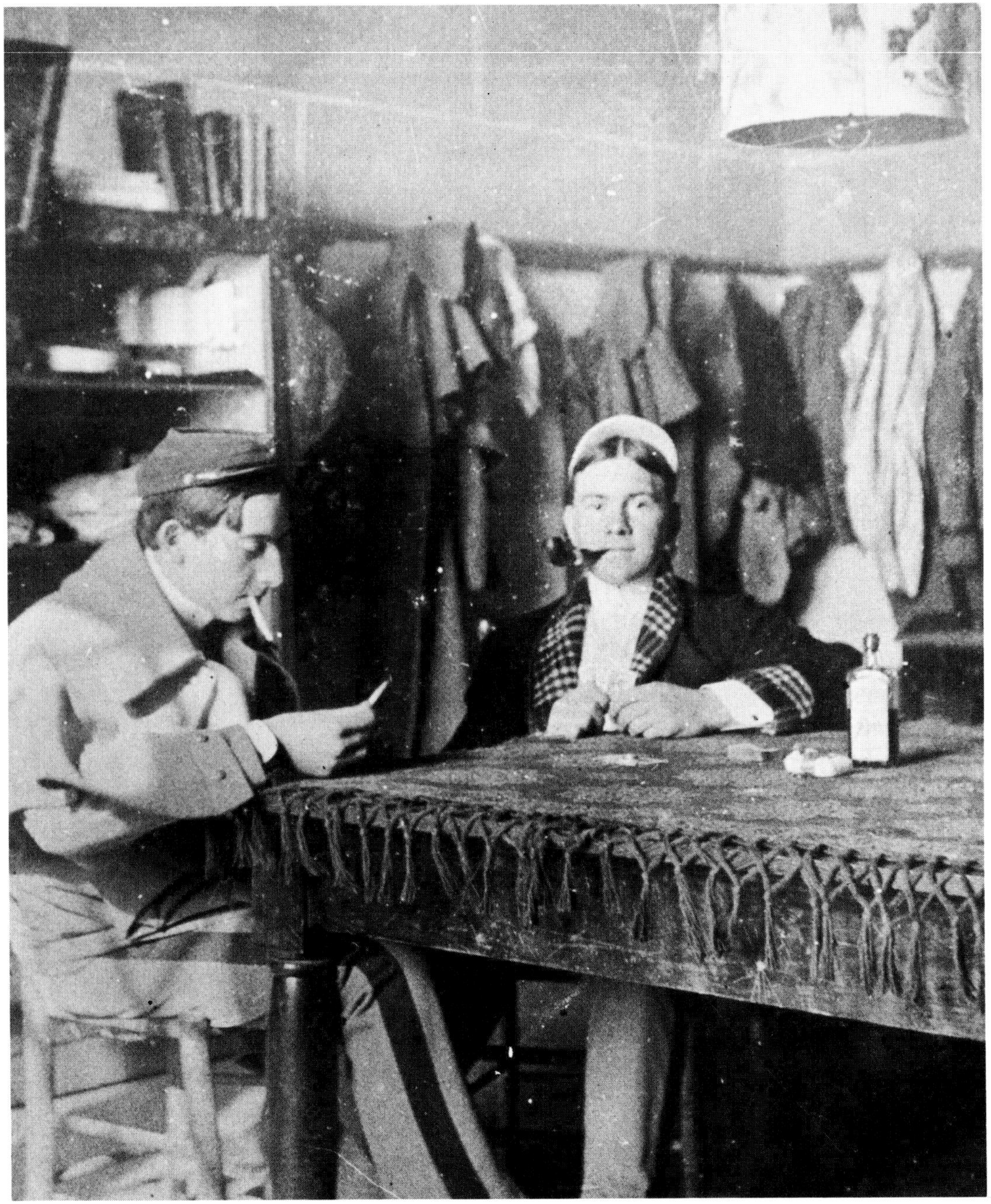

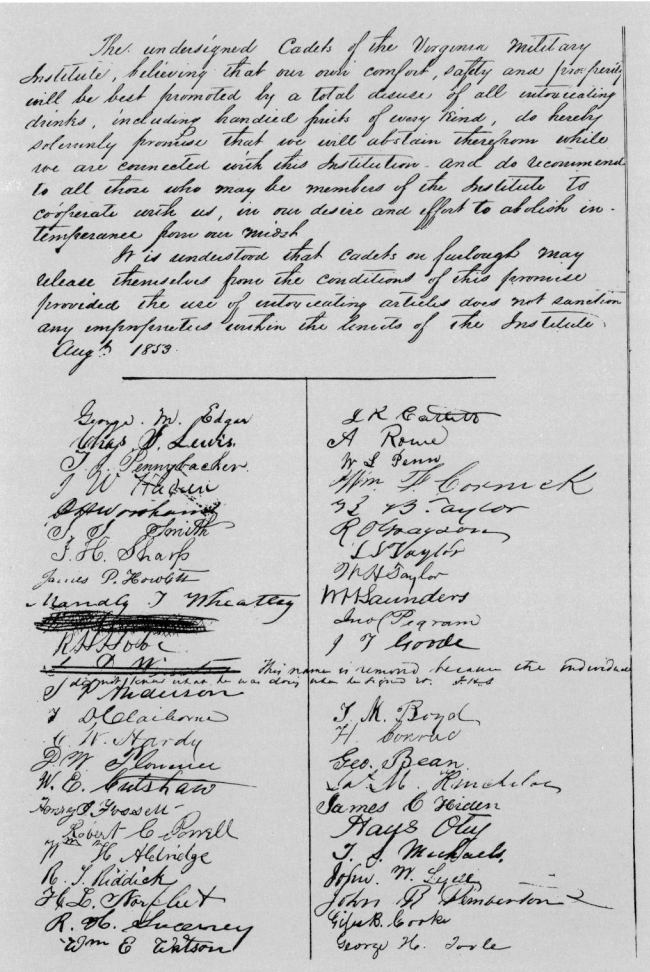

138

Roommates Joseph C. Allen and Herbert Tutwiler enjoy a friendly game of cards, c. 1902

"Two of my room mates . . . and myself—were sitting in my room, playing a social game at cards, a professor came to the door knocked and came in. We concealed our cards, as quick as possible, but not soon enough to escape. . . . The number of my demerits 'is rather my *misfortune* than my *fault*.' "

Cadet Joseph H. Chenoweth to his father, February 18, 1856

The undersigned Cadets of the Virginia Military Institute, believing that our own comfort, safety and prosperity will be best promoted by a total disuse of all intoxicating drinks, including brandied fruits of every kind, do hereby solemnly promise that we will abstain therefrom while we are connected with this Institution. and do recommend to all those who may be members of the Institute to cooperate with us, in our desire and effort to abolish intemperance from our midst.

It is understood that Cadets on furlough may release themselves from the conditions of this promise provided the use of intoxicating articles does not sanction any improprieties within the limits of the Institute.

Aug. 1853

George W. Edgar
Chas. F. Lewis
T. J. Pennybacker
J. W. Hazen
[illegible]
T. S. Smith
T. H. Sharp
James P. Howlett
Mandly T. Wheatley
[illegible]
R H Hobe
~~[illegible]~~ This name is removed because the individual did not know what he was doing when he signed it. F.H.S.
T. P. Anderson
T. D. Claiborne
C. W. Hardy
D. W. Flowree
W. E. Cutshaw
Henry J. Fossett
Robert C. Powell
Wm. H. Aldridge
R. T. Riddick
F. L. Norfleet
R. H. Sweeney
Wm. E. Watson

J K Cattett
A Rowe
W. L. Penn
Wm. F. Cormick
[illegible] Taylor
R O Grayson
L. T. Taylor
W. H. Taylor
W H Saunders
Jno. C Pegram
J T Goode
T. M. Boyd
H. Conrad
Geo. Bean
Ja. M. Hinchelo
James C Hiden
Hays Otey
T. S. Michaels
John W. Lyell
John R. Pemberton
Giles B. Cooke
George H. Toole

139

"Our own comfort, safety and prosperity will be best promoted by a total disuse of all intoxicating drinks. . . . It is understood that cadets on furlough may release themselves from the conditions of this promise." Temperance pledge, 1853

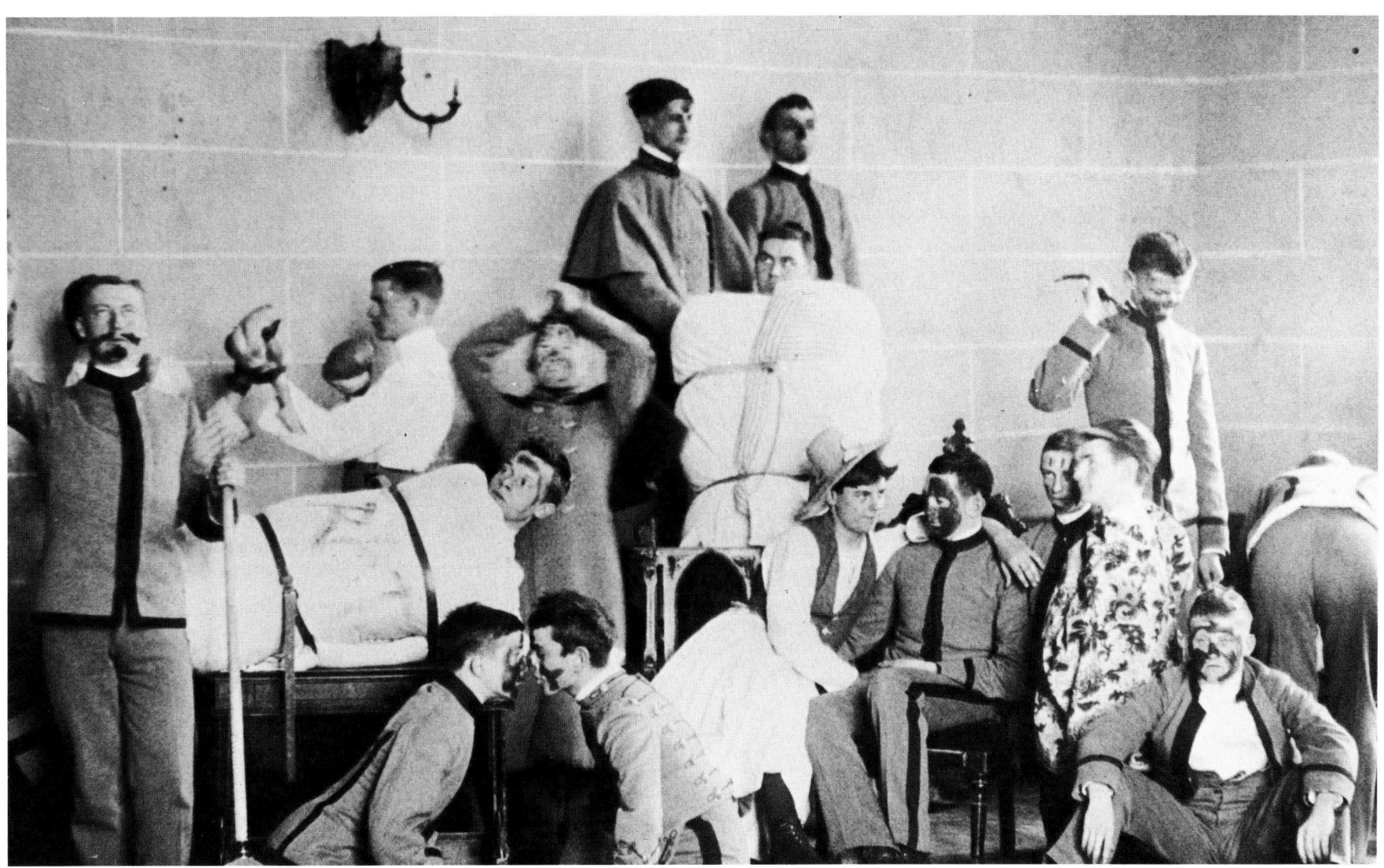

Antics in Barracks, c. 1892

"Cadet Jordan for absenting himself from Barracks, and visiting Lexington after retreat without authority, and in disguise, will forthwith return to his home under the provision of the Regulations applicable to such cases, & his connection with the Institute terminates with date."

Special order, June 14, 1867

> "Just before study drum the Arsenal was blown up with the rest of the 500 lbs. of powder. The Arsenal was entirely destroyed, the outside wall was entirely destroyed except the four corners. The Detective force is at work."
>
> *From diary of Thomas J. Nottingham, December 2, 1884*

141

The "Molly McGuires," c. 1890. Secret societies and fraternities appeared at VMI in the late 1860s. Three national social fraternities, Alpha Tau Omega, Kappa Sigma Kappa, and Sigma Nu, were founded by VMI cadets. Cadets later formed clandestine organizations such as the notorious "Molly McGuires," who are generally credited with blowing up the magazine. Hazings, bombings, and the belief that allegiance to these groups undermined the military discipline of the Institute led the Board of Visitors to outlaw both fraternities and secret societies in the late 1880s. The "Mollies," however, lived on in defiance of the ban.

An Average of the Measurements of the First Class

SHOWING INCREASE FOR THE FOUR YEARS

ON ENTRANCE.		ON GRADUATION.		INCREASE.	
Chest,	32.9 inches	Chest (normal),	35.5 inches	Chest,	2.6 inches
Weight,	137 pounds	Total Expansion of Chest,	4.5 "	Height,	2⅔ "
Height,	5 feet 8 inches	Expansion above normal,	2. "	Weight,	16 pounds
Waist	27.8 "	Biceps,	12.25 "	Waist,	0.6 inches
		Forearm,	11.9 "		
		Neck,	15. "		
		Hips,	37.1 "		
		Thigh,	20.25 "		
		Calf,	13.7 "		
		Height,	5 feet 10½ "		
		Weight,	153 pounds		
		Waist,	28.4 inches		

142

From The Bomb, *1895*

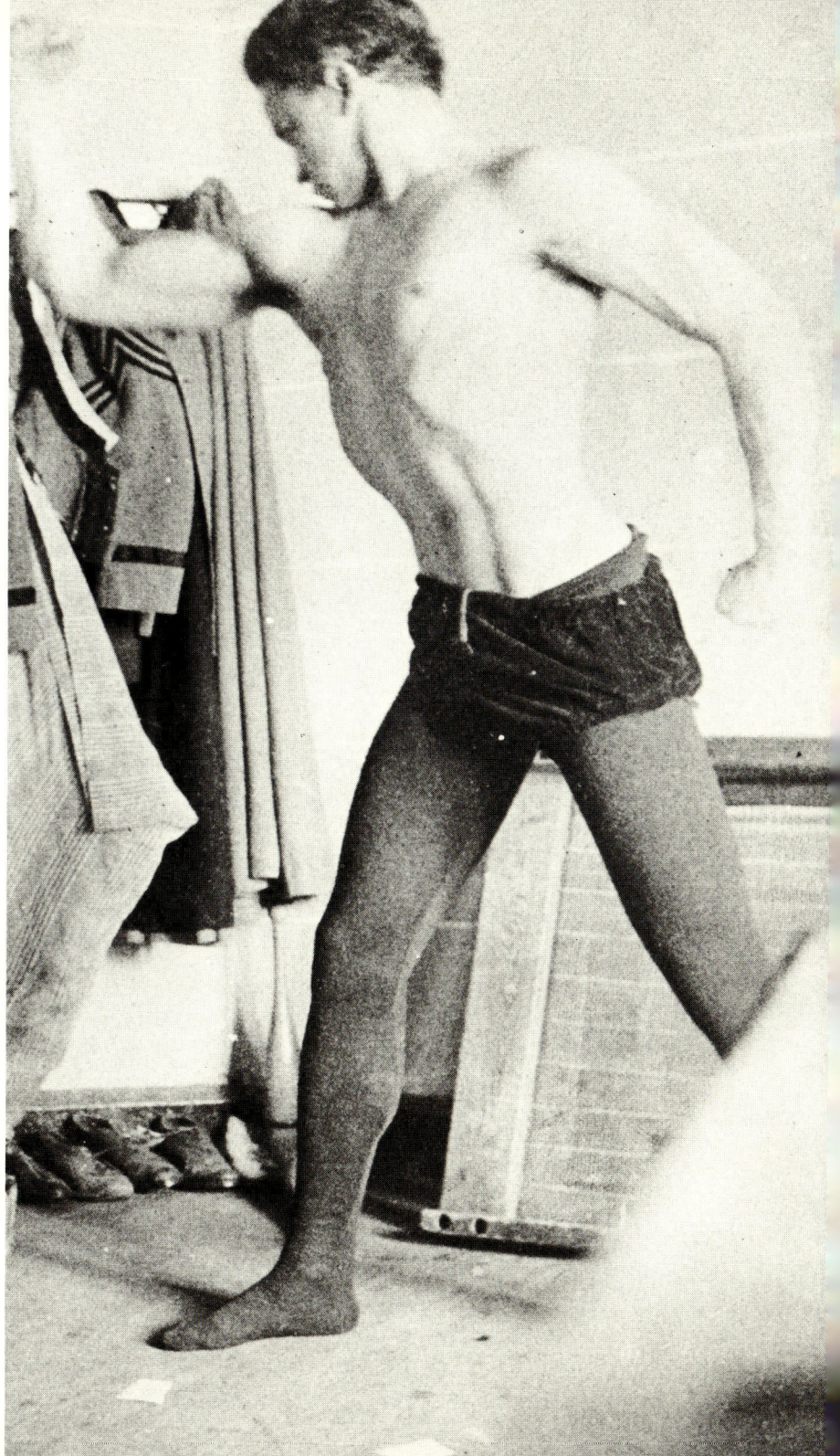

143

"Muscles" (c. 1907)

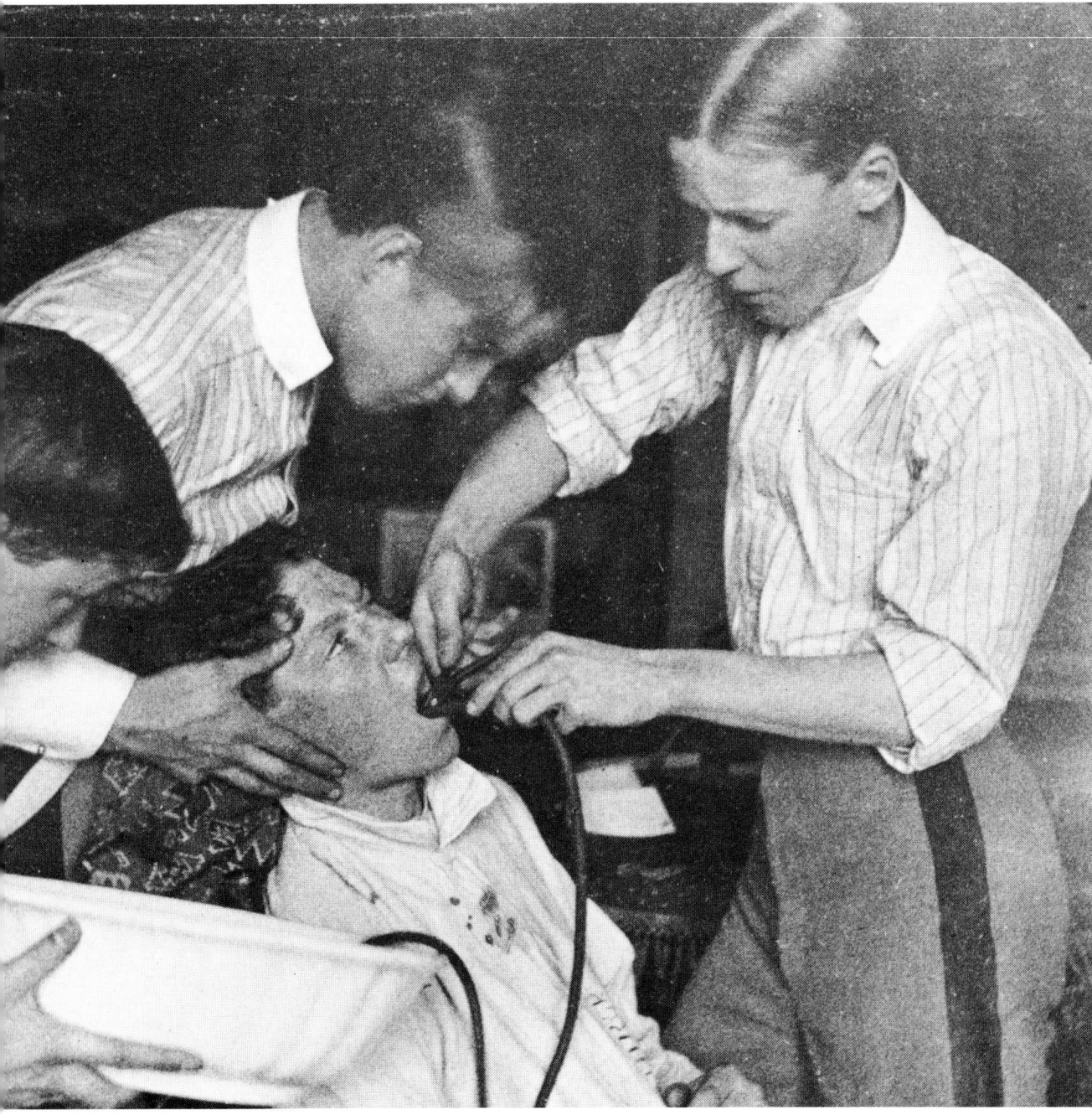

"Pulling a tooth" (c. 1900)

> "I went this morning to the Surgeon's office for the purpose of having one of my teeth extracted Dr. Estill pulled six times at it and succeeded in getting it all out except a part of the root. He immediately sent for a dentist who pulled at it twice, but could not get it out. He advised me to wait about a fortnight, in which time he thought the root would rise above the gum and enable him to get a hold on it. It was I believe the largest tooth in my head."

Cadet Charles A. Derby to his father, May 9, 1846

Blanket toss in camp, c. 1903

Appendix
Michael Miley, 1841–1918

An essay by Mame Warren, from the catalogue Michael Miley, American Photographer and Pioneer in Color: An Exhibition Presented by Washington and Lee University, DuPont Gallery, January 8–February 8, 1980. *Reprinted with permission of Washington and Lee University, Lexington, Virginia.*

PRIDE and prejudice, as has been noted elsewhere, often inspire strong emotion and exaggerated conviction. It should be no surprise, then, that Lexingtonians (and their Rockbridge County neighbors) believe that there were just two photographers in the last century of any real significance: Mathew Brady and Michael Miley.

Brady, of course, achieved his fame through his remarkable photographs of a war which to most minds is better forgotten. Miley, on the other hand, was a local boy who made good—very good—and did it all in the county itself.

The story that Miley, "General Lee's photographer" (no matter that Lee posed for Brady and for numerous others during the same period), had "discovered and developed color photography"[1] was already popular by the time his obituary was written in 1918. Not wholly true; but not entirely untrue, either.

Michael Miley was born July 19, 1841, in Rockingham County, Virginia. While he was still young, the family moved south to Rockbridge County, to a farm about three miles from Fairfield. At the age of nineteen, Miley went to war, serving in Gen. Thomas J. Jackson's "Stonewall Brigade."

When he returned to Lexington is not known for certain. It is certain that he began his photographic career after Appomattox, in Staunton, where he worked about a year with a Mr. Burdett. There, presumably, he learned to print positive images from collodion wet-plate glass negatives onto albumen-coated paper. He introduced this then-recently developed technique to Rockbridge County when he came to work for Andrew Plecker, a traveling photographer from Lynchburg.

Many "country photographers" at the time were experiencing difficulty with the process,[2] but the number and quality of the surviving Miley prints from this period suggest that he mastered it quickly. The new method required that plates be sensitized, exposed, and developed while wet. In contrast to daguerreotypes and tintypes, the new "wet" process made it possible to print any number of pictures from a single plate.

Plecker's was a transient operation; the two photographers, with all their equipment, a room for sittings, and a darkroom, traveled in his boxcar wagon. Miley's associa-

[1] Marshall Fishwick's very sympathetic book, *General Lee's Photographer* (University of North Carolina Press, 1954), is partly responsible for the exaggerated local reputation of Michael Miley today. But the obituary in the Lexington *Gazette* ("Death of Mr. Michael Miley Last Thursday Morning," May 29, 1918, p. 4) shows that the legend was already established then. Research has indicated that Miley's were probably the first successful colored photographic prints in the United States, but his process made little contribution to the development of color photography as we know it today.

[2] William Welling, *Photography in America: The Formative Years, 1839–1900* (New York: Thomas Crowell Co., 1978), p. 157.

tion with Plecker seems to have been brief, but it included at least one session—probably Miley's first—photographing Robert E. Lee, on Traveller, at Rockbridge Baths.

Late in 1866, Miley formed a partnership with Captain John C. Boude of Lexington; hence the stamp, "Boude and Miley," on early prints. The photography itself is attributable to Miley alone, however, since Boude is not known to have had any knowledge of or skill in photography; he was, instead, a business partner whose backing permitted Miley to open a studio and gallery on the corner of Main and Nelson streets, upstairs in the Hopkins Building.[3] In 1870, just prior to his marriage, Michael Miley bought out Boude's share in the business.

The studio was called The Stonewall Art Gallery, and, as the *Rockbridge County News* reported, "it became one of the sights of Lexington. Here were portraits of General Robert E. Lee and his family, to the third generation; of President Jefferson Davis, John C. Breckenridge, General Beauregard, Jubal Early, Commodore Maury, John Randolph Tucker, of all the professors in the University and Institute faculties . . . and many other notable men and women. All of these pictures were from sittings and a large portion were life size."[4]

Portraiture comprised the majority of Michael Miley's work. His famous images of Robert E. Lee were as popular then as they are now. In one of our primary sources about Miley's career, 22 pages of oral recollections transcribed in 1941, his son Henry commented that the picture of "General Lee on Traveller was the most salable photograph that Father made of him from direct life."[5] Lee himself requested that the photograph be made; he posed—in uniform for the first time—in the back garden of his home on the Washington College campus.

For many years, Miley had the annual assignment of documenting the classes and athletic teams at Washington and Lee University and at Virginia Military Institute. And so it was, though artist or subject could not have known it in 1901, that Miley photographed a cadet who was to become a great general, George C. Marshall.

In addition to his commercial work photographing brides, babies, and family groups, Michael Miley was intrigued with portraying beautiful women. Highly stylized poses were popular in such idealistic photography, and Miley's provided no exception. In his 1941 reminiscences, Henry Miley recalled more than a dozen "beautiful young ladies" from as far away as Kentucky who posed for his father's camera.[6] "He made a lot of photographs in his studio just because he considered the subject beautiful in some way and not because they came to have their pictures taken. One particular picture, the picture of a nun, was taken because he thought it would be outstanding. Another one was the picture of the girl with the basket of fruit on her head. These pictures were about 20-by-24 inches large."[7]

These negatives, on glass plates, were made with an enormous view camera. Despite its cumbersomeness and the auxiliary equipment needed to operate such a precision instrument, Miley did not hesitate to use it outside the studio as well as in. "He would always look out for any special picture," Henry Miley recalled. "He would get the carriage ready in a hurry if he saw that there was going to be a pretty cloud effect and rush down to the bend in North River before the cloud would leave. He wouldn't

---

[3]Boude, who was clerk of the County Court for many years, apparently entered into a similar arrangement at some other time with another photographer, as several prints in the Virginia Military Institute archives bear the label "Boude and McClelland."

[4]*Rockbridge County News*, "The Loss at Miley's," October 17, 1907, p. 5.

[5]Taken from p. 19 of "a verbatim transcript of conversations between Henry Miley, son and successor of his father Michael Miley, and Mr. Harrison Waddell, of Lexington, Va. The transcript was made by Mr. Waddell's secretary at his suggestion, in November, 1941, just before

---

Henry Miley left Lexington to live in other parts of the country. On a return visit in February, 1951, Mr. Miley stated that everything contained herein was (so far as he knew) correct and substantiated." A copy of the transcript is among the manuscripts in the Special Collections of the Washington and Lee University Library. It is hereafter referred to in these notes as Transcript.

[6]Ibid., p. 21.

[7]Ibid., p. 6.

waste any time getting set up, either."[8]

In 1907, tragedy struck the Miley firm when the studio and gallery were almost completely destroyed by fire. Negatives from 1885 on were lost; the early, more valuable negatives and most of the equipment, however, were saved. Several retail stores and the offices of the *Rockbridge County News* were also damaged severely by the fire. An acknowledgment of how dearly The Stonewall Art Gallery was cherished is evident in the newspaper's comment that "the loss of M. Miley & Son will appeal personally to more people than any other."[9]

The enterprise was far from lost, however. Two weeks later, a notice appeared in the paper that "our newly fitted up gallery ... opposite the courthouse is now ready for business."[10]

Michael Miley pursued all his interests with enthusiasm. On Sundays, he attended services at the Lexington Presbyterian Church twice, though he never joined the congregation. Toward the end of his life, he went to the movies almost every night to study the lighting effects.

But his house on White Street and his family were at the center of his affections. In 1870, he had married Martha Mackey, and they had three sons, Henry, Herbert, and Edwin. His niece, Frances Isabel Mackey Huffman, remembers that the Miley house was always full of people, and that there were flowers all year 'round. There were a greenhouse for exotic plants and a vegetable garden. "Uncle Miley—Mrs. Miley would not have him called 'Uncle Mike' because it sounded too Irish—gardened very scientifically."

"He used to get up early in the morning to go out and watch everything grow. Sometimes he would sit up nearly all night tending the fire to keep the greenhouse warm and things growing. We burned as much coal in the greenhouse as in the house," Henry recounted.[11]

Experimentation, whether in the greenhouse or in the darkroom, was always a challenge for Michael Miley. Though he traveled regularly to photographic conventions, he often did not wait for others' solutions to problems he was experiencing. Halation—fogging in negatives of high contrast—was a difficulty encountered by many photographers who used the new dry-plate process after 1880. Miley discovered the cause and began making his own plates with modifications to eliminate the troublesome reflections. Ten years later, plates similar to those devised by Miley were on the market.

In 1895, after graduation from Washington and Lee, Henry Miley joined his father as a partner in the business. About that time, Michael Miley became interested in carbon printing, a very difficult and time-consuming process. The technique, if properly carried out, results in a permanent print in any one color. Henry did much of the day-to-day commercial work, leaving his father free to work on his experiments.

The carbon process was enjoying a revival of interest in photographic circles with the introduction of a better carbon tissue, available in fifteen colors or shades.[12] Henry recalled in 1941: "It's such a difficult process that very few photographers ever undertook it. Carbon paper was not manufactured in the United States at that time, and not even today. It has to be gotten from London, England, so we ordered some from the Autotype Company, one roll each of red-chalk, sea-green, sepia, and black, and the transfer paper, with several 20-by-24-inch sheets of white celluloid, and started to learn the process of carbon printing. We undertook to make the first carbon print when the paper came in, and like everything Father did, he wanted to do it in a big way. He sensitized a 20-by-24 sheet of sepia carbon for our first print, in the darkroom, and tacked it on the back of the door. The paper pulled away from the door and fell to the floor, which was not very clean. We

---

[8]Ibid., p. 9.

[9]*Rockbridge County News*, "The Loss at Miley's," October 17, 1907, p. 5.

[10]Ibid., advertisement, November 7, 1907, p. 5.

[11]Transcript, p. 5.

[12]Welling, p. 351.

hung it up again, thinking it was spoiled, and when it was dry, we brushed the dust off and proceeded to make the print. Much to our surprise, the print turned out very good, and it was interesting to see the picture develop when that slimy brown mass was washed from the celluloid. We soon found out that the carbon printing was no easy process."[13]

Gradually, father and son began to consider the possibility of making full-color prints by superimposing the carbon images, using a primary color for each. It took them years to perfect the procedure. Finding materials of the proper quality and tone was difficult, since there was so little commercial demand for them.

"We wrote to the Autotype Company stating just how we would like to have the tri-color paper prepared, but they were not willing to undertake it at first as it was very expensive and there was no demand for it. We tried to make our own paper but were not successful. The Autotype Company must have gotten interested finally, for [in] the summer of 1900 they sent us one roll of each color, red, yellow, and blue.... We soon found it was delicate, uncertain, and hard work. Sometimes the pictures were very good and then again the colors would not be quite true to the original picture. It seemed to be impossible to get a color, as pure red or green, to photograph as it should. We felt there was a mistake somewhere."[14]

They persevered, however, and in 1902 were issued a patent on the process.[15] In 1905, the Franklin Institute awarded Michael and Henry Miley a medal of merit. Quite probably, they had produced the first colored photographic prints on paper in the United States.[16]

In all, Michael and Henry Miley produced about five hundred color prints. Their subjects were mostly still lifes and copies of paintings, since these could be controlled and the color checked accurately. One of the most popular was of Charles Willson Peale's portrait of George Washington, in the Custis Lee Collection of Washington and Lee University. Miley photographed all the paintings in the collection, as well as the then-just-completed mural of the Battle of New Market, in Jackson Hall at Virginia Military Institute. These color prints have retained their strong, deep tones even to today, and seem to be less subject to fading than modern color prints.

Yet despite the significance of his color experiments, and despite popular belief, Michael Miley is almost unknown in the annals of photography. The reason may have been suggested in his obituary: "In his experiments, Mr. Miley made remarkable discoveries in the art of applying color to photography and made many exquisite pictures in color. His discovery was patented but he looked upon the process as too slow and costly for commercial purposes and made no effort to have it brought into general use."[17]

In this exhibition, then, which brings together for the first time prints that show the development of his talent, his diversity, his artistry, and his technical achievement, Washington and Lee University hopes to help right the balance and place the name of Michael Miley more securely in the history of American photography.

December 14, 1979

---

[13] Transcript, pp. 13–14.

[14] Transcript, pp. 15–16.

[15] The Mileys' application for their patent, which includes very specific details on how the process was accomplished, is printed as Appendix III in Fishwick, pp. 90–94.

[16] The local misconception that Michael Miley "invented" color photography probably arises from confusion about photographic techniques. Welling points to the work of French experimenter Ducos du Hauron, who in 1869 "proposed three different ways in which to reconstitute [i.e., obtain] colored images, either for viewing or in print form" (p. 200). His ideas—very similar to Miley's—were accomplished in Europe by 1877. In Europe and in the United States, others as well were testing various theories, with varying degrees of success. By 1894, both F. E. Ives and Robert D. Graves had perfected methods for momentary viewing of superimposed color images on a screen (pp. 359–61).

[17] *Rockbridge County News*, "Mr. Michael Miley Died at 2 O'clock This Morning," May 23, 1918, p. 4.

Key to Illustrations and Quotations

Unless otherwise noted, all materials are located in the VMI Archives. For photographs, the photographer, size of original, and photograph accession number are given; for personal papers, the collection name is given; and for official records, the Record Group (RG) name.

Front cover: Boude & Miley, 4 x 2½, no. 221-26 (Album).
Front endleaf: Michael Miley, 19¼ x 8½, no. 2157.
P. i: RG Office of Cadet Affairs, Invitations File.
P. ii: Photographer unknown, 4¾ x 3¾, no. 229 (Album of Raymond V. Hess, Class of 1906). Donor: Mrs. Kathryn T. DelaCourt.
P. iv: RG Commandant, Band Records. Cover from sheet music by Edward Steinmueller, a member of the VMI band, 1888–1903.
P. v: Miller Studio (Lexington and Buena Vista), 8½ x 5¼, no. 440.
P. vi: Thomas W. Keitt Collection. Pen and ink with color wash, 15½ x 12.
P. viii: Photographer unknown, 4¾ x 3¾, no. 229 (Album of Raymond V. Hess, Class of 1906). Donor: Mrs. Kathryn T. DelaCourt.
P. xi: Michael Miley, 8½ x 6½, no. 285 (Album).
P. xii: Photographer unknown, 9 x 11, no. 253. Donor: William Nalle.
P. xiii: RG Dean of the Faculty, Registrar's Records.
Illus. 1: Michael Miley, 4 x 8, no. 1998. Thomas Hoomes Williamson, a faculty member from 1841 to 1887, is generally credited with designing the Limit Gates.
Illus. 2: Charles P. Dorman Collection. From a contemporary copy of the act.
Quotation, p. 2: Valentine C. Saunders Collection. donor: DeButts Saunders.
Illus. 3: Diploma/Certificate Collection (oversized). Lithograph from a Cadet Dialectic Society Certificate.
Illus. 5: G. W. Minnis (Richmond), 2½ x 4, no. 1856, signed.
Quotation, p. 4: RG Superintendent, Incoming Correspondence, 1841.
Illus. 6: Photographer unknown, 2¾ x 3¼, no. 1863, daguerreotype.
Quotation, p. 5: RG Board of Visitors.
Illus. 7: Michael Miley, 8 x 4, no. 307. Donor: Hugh D. Wise, Class of 1891.
Illus. 8: Boude & Miley, 14 x 10½, no. 1851.
Illus. 9: RG Dean of the Faculty, Registrar's Records.
Illus. 10: Photographer unknown, 2¾ x 3¼ no. 2151, daguerreotype.
Illus. 11: Russell Pancake Collection. Donor: Richard F. Harmison.

Illus. 12: Photographer unknown, 2¾ x 3¼, ambrotype, original housed in VMI Museum.
Illus. 13: James H. Waddell Collection. Pencil sketch, 5 x 7½. Donor: Edward C. Shepherd III.
Illus. 14: RG Superintendent, Order Book, Nov. 1839–Jan. 1852.
Illus. 15: Photographer unknown, 2¾ x 3¼, ambrotype, original housed in VMI Museum. Donor: Mrs. Juliet Goode Thomas.
Illus. 16: Boude & Miley, 2½ x 4, no. 2139, signed.
Illus. 17: Photographer unknown, 2¾ x 3¼, ambrotype, original housed in VMI Museum. Donor: Miss Elizabeth Gisiner.
Quotation, p. 13: RG Superintendent, Order Book, Jan. 1861–August 1863.
Illus. 19: Moses Ezekiel Collection. Pen and ink sketch, 3 x 4 on 8 x 11 paper. Donor: Mrs. Albert E. Rauh.
Illus. 20: Boude & Miley, 7½ x 5½ oval in 10 x 8 mat, no. 1053. Donor: J. S. Bagnall.
Quotation, p. 16: John L. Tunstall Collection. Donor: Alexander L. Tunstall.
Illus. 21: Jaqueline Beverly Stanard Collection.
Illus. 22: Photographer unknown, 5½ x 7½, no. 039. Donor: Mrs. Parke Houston.
Illus. 23: Photographer unknown, 4¾ x 3¾, no. 229 (Album of Raymond V. Hess, Class of 1906). Donor: Mrs. Kathryn T. DelaCourt.
Illus. 24: Photographer unknown, 4¾ x 6¾, no. 229 (Album of Raymond V. Hess, Class of 1906). Donor: Mrs. Kathryn T. DelaCourt.
Quotation, p. 18: RG Surgeon, Special Report.
Illus. 25: Andrew H. Plecker, 4 x 2½, no. 220-19 (Album of John B. Gray, Class of 1867). Michael Miley worked briefly for Plecker, a traveling photographer from Lynchburg. Donor: Miss Aylmer Gray.
Quotation, p. 18: Sidney Marlin Collection.
Illus. 26: Michael Miley, 4 x 5½, no. 1314.
Quotation, p. 19: William Nalle Collection. Donor: William Nalle.
Illus. 27: Michael Miley, 2½ x 4¼, no. 2152. Donor: James L. White, from the estate of Mrs. Frank R. White.
Illus. 28: W. E. Rippey (Parkersburg, W. Va.), 2½ x 4, no. 221-33 (Album), inscribed.
Illus. 29: Michael Miley, 7¼ x 5½ on 10 x 8 mat, no. 2160. *Left to right:* Robert L. Pollard, Jack F. Ross, Frank T. Blakemore, Samuel W. Washington, John Loney. Donor: C. Donald Stegman.
Illus. 30: Michael Miley, 4 x 2½, no. 224-46 (Album).
Illus. 31: Michael Miley, 4 x 2½, no. 224-45 (Album).
Illus. 32: Miley cartouche, 2¾ x 4¾. From reverse of F. H. Smith's photo, no. 272 (Album).
Illus. 33: Michael Miley, 11 x 14, no. 2153. Donor: Keitt Purcell.

Illus. 34: Photographer unknown, 10 x 8 on 14 x 10½ mat, no. 1854. Donor: Thornton T. Perry.
Illus. 36: RG Commandant, Guard Records.
Illus. 37: Thomas J. Nottingham Collection. Donor: Edward Ferebee.
Illus. 38: Michael Miley, 4 x 7½, no. 2132. Donor: Sallie Aylett Goodwyn.
Illus. 39: Archives, printed materials.
Illus. 40: Photographer unknown, 19 x 11, no. 1850. Donor: Mattie Purcell.
Illus. 41: RG Office of Cadet Affairs, Invitations file.
Illus. 42: Michael Miley, 15 x 20 on 20 x 24 mat, no. 180.
Illus. 43: Photographer unknown, 6½ x 4¼, no. 157. Part of the Class of 1894 as fourth classmen. *Right to left: (upper row)* Warren G. Elliott, Graves M. Moses, Charles C. Berkeley; *(middle row)* William Steenbergen, William L. Daughtrey, Philip St. George Cocke, Mosely S. Dickinson, William M. Blocher (ex-classmate), Cary D. Langhorne; *(bottom row)* Benjamin O. Blackford, Charles T. Beale, Arthur S. Hines.
Illus. 44: Miller Studio (Lexington and Buena Vista), 10 x 7, no. 2010 (detail).
Illus. 45: RG Office of Cadet Affairs, Cadet Publications. Volume I, No. 3, p. 85. The *Cadet* was published from March 1871 through January 1873 and was briefly revived in the 1890s. The student newspaper of the same title was started in 1907 and still retains the name.
Illus. 46: Photographer unknown, 9¼ x 7½ on 12 x 10 mat, no. 2155. Donor: Walter H. Taylor.
Illus. 47: Michael Miley, 17 x 11 on 22 x 17 mat, no. 178.
Illus. 48: Photographer unknown, 5½ x 6¼, no. 1039. Donor: William P. Upshur.
Illus. 49: Conway Howard Collection. Donor: Jeanne C. Howard.
Illus. 50: Photographer unknown, 9½ x 7¼ on 13 x 11 mat, no. 2077.
Illus. 52: Photographer unknown, 6¾ x 4¾, no. 229 (Album of Raymond V. Hess, Class of 1906). Donor: Mrs. Kathryn T. DelaCourt.
Illus. 53: RG Superintendent.
Quotations, pp. 38, 39, 42, 57, 61, 65, 66: Edward Minor Watson Collection. Donor: Mrs. William C. Watson.
Illus. 54: Michael Miley, 8 x 5, no. 160, Donor: H. W. Reynolds.
Illus. 55: Photographer unknown, 3¼ x 3¼, no. 1037.
Illus. 56: RG Superintendent, Order Book, Nov. 1839–Jan. 1852.
Illus. 57: Photographer unknown, 3¼ x 2¼, no. 2137 (Album of Harding Polk, Class of 1907). Donor: Gen. James H. Polk.

Illus. 58: Charles Balmer, Jr., Collection.
Illus. 59: Photographer unknown, 4¼ x 4, no. 1456.
Illus. 60: Photographer unknown, 2¼ x 3¼, no. 2137 (Album of Harding Polk, Class of 1907). Donor: Gen. James H. Polk.
Illus. 61: Photographer unknown, 6¾ x 4¾, no. 229 (Album of Raymond V. Hess, Class of 1906). Donor: Mrs. Kathryn T. DelaCourt.
Illus. 62: RG Dean of the Faculty, Registrar's Records.
Illus. 63: Cartoon by unknown cadet; photographed by Michael Miley, 9 x 6¼ on 12 x 10 mat, no. 2162.
Illus. 64: RG Dean of the Faculty, Registrar's Records.
Illus. 65: Michael Miley, 2½ x 4¼, no. 131.
Illus. 66: Edward L. Smith Collection. Pen and ink with color wash, 14 x 9.
Illus. 67: Michael Miley, 8 x 4, no. 1940.
Illus. 68: Michael Miley, 8 x 4, no. 394. Donor: Hugh D. Wise, Class of 1891.
Illus. 69: A. J. Davis Collection. Drawing no. 12. Pen and ink with color wash, 11 x 14.
Illus. 70: RG Treasurer.
Quotation, p. 48: RG Commandant, Incoming Correspondence, 1865.
Illus. 71: Robert E. Lee Map Collection. Map no. 15. 26 x 19, signed. Donor: G. W. C. Lee.
Illus. 72: Boude & Miley, 2½ x 4, no. 221-10 (Album).
Illus. 73: Photographer unknown, 5¼ x 4¼, no. 370.
Illus. 74: Boude & Miley, 2½ x 4, no 118.
Illus. 75: Wayland (Cambridge, Eng.), 2½ x 4, no. 221-13 (Album).
Illus. 76: Joseph H. Chenoweth Collection. Donor: Roy Bird Cook.
Illus. 77: Michael Miley, 10¼ x 13½ on 13 x 16 mat, no. 192.
Illus. 78: Photographer unknown, 4¾ x 3¾, no. 1042.
Illus. 79: Photographer unknown, 6¾ x 4¾, no. 229 (Album of Raymond V. Hess, Class of 1906). Donor: Mrs. Kathryn T. DelaCourt.
Illus. 80: Edward C. Shepherd Collection. Pen and ink with color wash, 14 x 9. Donor: Edward C. Shepherd III.
Illus. 81: Michael Miley, 4¼ x 6½, no. 272 (Album).
Illus. 82: RG Dean of the Faculty, Registrar's Records. From the *Register of Officers and Cadets*.
Illus. 83: Photographer unknown, 3¼ x 2¼, no. 2137 (Album of Harding Polk, Class of 1907). Donor: Gen. James H. Polk.
Illus. 84: Photographer unknown, 4½ x 3½ on 6½ x 5½ mat, no. 1454.
Illus. 85: Michael Miley, 23 x 19 on 32 x 28 mat, no. 1778. *Left to right: (seated)* E. W. Nichols, J. M. Brooke, Superintendent Shipp, T. M. Semmes, R. A. Marr; *(standing)* N. B. Tucker, T. R. Marshall, J. S. Parke, H. Pendleton.
Illus. 86: Photographer unknown, 6¾ x 4¾, no. 229 (Album of Raymond V. Hess, Class of 1906). Donor: Mrs. Kathryn T. DelaCourt.
Illus. 87: Photographer unknown, 6¾ x 4¾, no. 229 (Album of Raymond V. Hess, Class of 1906). Donor: Mrs. Kathryn T. DelaCourt.
Illus. 88: Michael Miley, 8½ x 6, no. 1836.
Illus. 89: Photographer unknown, 5 x 4, no. 1907. Donor: Ida B. Routh.
Illus. 90: Photographer unknown, 5½ x 6½, no. 1911. Donor: Louise A. Illig.
Quotation, p. 59: RG Superintendent, Order Book, Sept. 1866–June 1876.
Illus. 91: Michael Miley, 8½ x 5, no. 249. Donor: Family of William Nalle.
Illus. 92: RG Commandant, Guard Records.
Illus. 93: Photographer unknown, 6¾ x 4¾, no. 229 (Album of Raymond V. Hess, Class of 1906). Donor: Mrs. Kathryn T. DelaCourt.
Illus. 94: Michael Miley, 4 x 2½, no. 224-47 (Album).
Illus. 95: Page 93.
Quotation, p. 62: Edmund Berkeley Collection.
Illus. 96: Michael Miley, 4¼ x 6½, no. 282 (Album).
Illus. 97: RG Board of Visitors, Minutes.
Illus. 98: Photographer unknown, 4 x 3, no. 227.
Illus. 99: H. C. Mann, 8 x 10, no. 1614.
Illus. 100: RG Public Information Office, Viewbook, 1910.
Illus. 101: Photographer unknown, 6 x 8¾ on 8 x 10 mat, no. 252. Donor: Mrs. Hardin W. Reynolds.
Illus. 102: RG Commandant, Guard Records.
Illus. 103: Photographer unknown, 3¼ x 2¼, no. 2137 (Album of Harding Polk, Class of 1907). Donor: Gen. James H. Polk.
Quotation, p. 67: Charles M. Barton Collection. Donor: Lewis N. Barton.
Illus. 104: RG Commandant, Demerit Book.
Illus. 105: Miller Studio (Lexington and Buena Vista), 8½ x 5¼, no. 374. Donor: John Wise, Class of 1902.
Illus. 106: Page 142.
Quotation, p. 69: Samuel F. Atwill Collection. Donor: William H. Atwill.
Illus. 107: Michael Miley, 13½ x 10 on 17 x 12 mat, no. 2159.
Illus. 108: Michael Miley, 4½ x 3½, no. 278 (Album).
Illus. 109: Miller Studio (Lexington and Buena Vista), 8½ x 5¼, no. 377.
Illus. 110: Page 111.
Illus. 111: Photographer unknown, 22½ x 16½, no. 179.
Quotation, p. 72: RG Office of Cadet Affairs, *The Bullet*. Written by T. Croxton Gordon, Class of 1904.
Illus. 112: Michael Miley, 22½ x 17½, no. 383.
Illus. 113: Page 97.
Illus. 114: Photographer unknown, 13 x 9 on 14 x 10 mat, no. 201.
Illus. 115: Conway Howard Collection. Donor: Jeanne C. Howard.
Illus. 117 and 118: Conway Howard Collection. Donor: Jeanne C. Howard.
Illus. 119: Photographer unknown, 3 x 5¼, no. 308-70 (Album of Alonzo H. Gentry, Class of 1908). Donor: Mrs. A. H. Gentry.
Illus. 120: Nellie Gibbs Collection. Donor: Nellie Gibbs.
Illus. 121: Michael Miley, 4 x 6¼, no. 379.
Illus. 122: Photographer unknown, 9½ x 6½ on 14 x 11 mat, no. 169. Club members are listed in the 1895 *Bomb*.
Illus. 123: Page 156.
Illus. 124: Photographer unknown, 3 x 2¼, no. 2137 (Album of Harding Polk, Class of 1907). Donor: Gen. James H. Polk.
Illus. 125: RG Superintendent, Order Book, Jan. 1885–March 1891.
Illus. 126: Photographer unknown, 3¾ x 2¼, no. 1500-84 (Album).
Illus. 127: Photographer unknown, 6¾ x 4¾, no. 229 (Album of Raymond V. Hess, Class of 1906). Donor: Mrs. Kathryn T. DelaCourt.
Quotation, p. 81: Charles T. Haigh Collection. Donor: John L. Dillard.
Illus. 128: RG Office of Cadet Affairs, Invitations File.
Illus. 129: Photographer unknown, 3¼ x 3¼, no. 308-133 (Album of Alonzo H. Gentry, Class of 1908). Donor: Mrs. A. H. Gentry.
Illus. 130: RG Office of Cadet Affairs, Invitations File.
Illus. 131: Photographer unknown, 7 x 5, no. 1152. Donor: John Wise, Class of 1895.
Quotation, p. 83: RG Superintendent, Incoming Correspondence, 1842.
Illus. 133: Photographer unknown, 4¾ x 4 on 6½ x 5½ mat, no. 2184. The Misses Roller were daughters of John E. Roller, Class of 1863. Donor: Mrs. Margaret Weaver.
Illus. 134: Photographer unknown, 4½ x 2½, no. 308-127 (Album of Alonzo H. Gentry, Class of 1908). Donor: Mrs. A. H. Gentry.
Illus. 135: RG Superintendent, Order Book, July 1857–Dec. 1860.
Quotation, p. 85: Philip C. Gibbs Collection.
Illus. 136: RG Superintendent, Order Book, Nov. 1839–Jan. 1852.
Illus. 137: Miller Studio (Lexington and Buena Vista), 5¾ x 4¼, no. 289 (Album). *Left to right: (front row)* Mosley S. Dickinson, Henry A. Wise; *(back row)* Charles B. Coffeen, Douglas B. Smith, James M. S. Waring, Harry E. Biscoe. All were members of the Class of 1894. Donor: Henry A. Wise.
Illus. 138: Photographer unknown, 6¼ x 5¼, no. 1040. Donor: William P. Upshur.
Quotation, p. 86: Joseph H. Chenoweth Collection. Donor: Roy Bird Cook.
Illus. 139: RG Superintendent, Order Book, Jan. 1852–July 1857.
Illus. 140: Michael Miley, 8 x 5, no. 155.
Quotation, p. 87: RG Superintendent, Order Book, Dec. 1865–July 1867.

Quotation, p. 88: Thomas J. Nottingham Collection. Donor: Edward Ferebee.
Illus. 141: Photographer unknown, 8 x 5, no. 256. Donor: Mrs. H. W. Reynolds.
Illus. 142: Page 57.
Illus. 143: Photographer unknown, 3¼ x 4, no. 2156 (Album of Robert C. Barrett, Class of 1907).

Illus. 144: Photographer unknown, 4¼ x 3½, no. 228 (Album of Alfred P. Upshur, Class of 1904). *Left to right: (standing)* Alfred P. Upshur, Sidney A. Loughridge, William H. Langhorne; *(seated)* Clement B. Lathrop. All were members of the Class of 1904.
Quotation, p. 90: Charles A. Derby Collection. Donor: Mrs. Margaret S. Clark.
Illus. 145: Photographer unknown, 6¾ x 4¾, no. 229 (Album of Raymond V. Hess, Class of 1906). Donor: Mrs. Kathryn T. DelaCourt.
Back endleaf: Michael Miley, 7¾ x 4, no. 1939. Donor: Hugh D. Wise, Class of 1891.
Back cover: The *Bomb* (1885), page 89.

Name Index

VMI Class designation appears in parentheses immediately after the name. Page numbers appear in roman type; illustration numbers are in italic type. An asterisk (*) following an index entry indicates that the Key to Illustrations and Quotations should be consulted for information not contained in a photograph's caption.

Allen, Joseph C. (1902), *48, 138*
Atwill, Samuel F. (1866 NM), 69

Balmer Jr., Charles (1886), *58*
Barton, Charles M. (1856), 67
Beale, Charles T. (1894), *43**
Berkeley, Charles C. (1894), *43**
Berkeley, Edmund (1867 NM), 62
Biscoe, Harry E. (1894), *109, 137**
Blackford, Benjamin O. (1894), *43**
Blakemore, Frank T. (1874), *29**
Blocher, William M. (1895), *43**
Bowen, Walter (1843), 83
Boyd, Waller M. (1863), *15, 104*
Brooke, John M., *74, 77, 85**
Browne, William T. (1844), 4

Chenoweth, Joseph H. (1859), *76, 86*
Clark, Gaylord B. (1867 NM), 22
Cocke, Philip St. George (1894), *43**
Coffeen, Charles B. (1894), *137**

Daughtrey, William L. (1894), *43**
Davis, Alexander Jackson, 67, 68, 69, 70
Derby, Charles A. (1848), 90
DeVault, Albert B. (1908), *119*
Dickinson, Mosely S. (1894), *43*, 137**
Dinwiddie, Hardaway H. (1867 NM), 22

Elliott Jr., Warren G. (1894), *43**

George, Robert C. (1887), *121*
Gibbs, Philip C. (1851), 85

Gisiner, John T. D. (1865), 17
Goode, Edward B. (1862), 15

Haigh, Charles T. (1866), 81
Hardin, Mark B. (1858), 77
Hardy, Charles W. (1857), 12
Hayes, Thomas G. (1867 NM), 22
Hines, Arthur S. (1894), *43**

Illig, John, *90*

Jackson, Thomas J. ("Stonewall"), *18, 19, 20, 63*
Keitt, Thomas W. (1878), vi

Langhorne, Cary D. (1894), *43**
Langhorne, William H. (1904), *144**
Lathrop, Clement B. (1904), *144**
Lawrason, Samuel M. (1872), xii
Lee, G. W. Custis, 72
Lee, Robert E., 26, 71
Loney, John (1873), *29**
Loughridge, Sidney A. (1904), *144**
Lyell, John W. (1859), 77

Madison, Robert L., 18, 77
Marlin, Sidney, 18
Marr, Robert A. (1877), *78, 85**
Marshall, George C. (1901), *112*
Marshall, Thomas R. (1879), *85**
Maury, Matthew F., 75
McDonald, Marshall (1860), 77
Morrison, James H. (1860), 77
Moses, Graves M. (1894), *43**

Nalle, William (1872), 19
Nichols, Edward W. (1878), 85
Nottingham, Thomas J. (1886), *37, 88*

Owens, Simon K. (1888), *121*

Pancake, Russell, *11*
Parke, John S., *85**
Patton, William M. (1865 NM), 77
Payne, Patrick, *96*
Pendleton, Hunter, *85**
Poindexter, Richard N. (1895), *109*
Pollard, Robert L. (1874), *29**
Preston, John T. L., 4, 5

Redfield, James M. (1887), *121*
Rockenbach, Samuel D. (1889), *121*
Roller, Frances L., *133*
Roller, Margaret S., *133*
Ross, Jack F. (1873), *29**

Saunders, Valentine (1842), 2
Semmes, Thomas M. (1860), *77, 85**
Shepherd, Edward C. (1855), 80
Shipp, Scott (1859), *16, 77, 85*
Smith, Alexander H. (1870), 28
Smith, Douglas H. (1894), *109, 137**
Smith, Edward L. (1856), 66
Smith, Francis H., 5, 77, 81
Stanard, Jaqueline B. (1867 NM), *21*
Steenbergen, William (1894), *43**

Terry, Thornton (1887), *38*
Tucker, Nathaniel B. (1888), *85*, 121*
Tunstall, John L. (1867 NM), 22
Tutwiler, Edward M. (1867 NM), 22
Tutwiler, Herbert (1902), *138*

Upshur, Alfred P. (1904), *144**
Upshur, William P. (1902), *48*

Waddell, James H. (1855), 13
Waring, James M. S. (1894), *137**
Washington, Samuel W. (1873), *29**
Watson, Edward M. (1871), *38, 39, 42, 57, 61, 65, 66*
Williamson, Thomas H., 65, 77
Wise, Henry A. (1894), *137**

98